Preparing for Sunday

Preparing for Sunday

Exploring the Readings for Year A

John Spicer, CSsR

NOVALIS

© 2004 Novalis, Saint Paul University, Ottawa, Canada

Cover: Suzanne Latourelle
Layout: Caroline Gagnon, Richard Proulx

Business Office:
Novalis
49 Front Street East, 2nd Floor
Toronto, Ontario, Canada
M5E 1B3

Phone: 1-800-387-7164 or (416) 363-3303
Fax: 1-800-204-4140 or (416) 363-9409
E-mail: cservice@novalis.ca
www.novalis.ca

National Library of Canada Cataloguing in Publication

Spicer, J. E. (John Ewart), 1919–
    Preparing for Sunday : exploring the readings for year
A / J.E. Spicer.

ISBN 2-89507-523-9

    1. Bible–Liturgical lessons, English. 2. Church year
meditations.
3. Catholic Church–Prayer-books and devotions–English.
I. Title.

BS390.S64 2004   264'.029   C2004-902622-4

Printed in Canada.

We acknowledge the financial support of the Government
of Canada through the Book Publishing Industry Develop-
ment Program (BPIDP) for our publishing activities.

Contents

Preface

Near the beginning of my priestly ministry, I gathered groups of people to reflect on our faith. I was amazed at the sense of togetherness that these groups experienced and also at the valuable insights they expressed and shared.

In 1968, Archbishop Jordan asked me to head a new commission in the Archdiocese of Edmonton: Adult Religious Education (a first in Canada). I began by writing reflection booklets on the documents of Vatican II, and then went on to produce bible reflection booklets and guidelines on Mark, Matthew, Luke/Acts, John and Revelation. These were well received.

More recently, I wrote reflection booklets for all three cycles of Sunday readings. Both groups and individuals in the Archdiocese found these booklets very helpful as they explore their faith.

Preparing for Sunday: Exploring the Readings for Year A grew out of these reflection booklets and will now reach a wider audience. I am convinced that readers' insights, together with those offered here, will lead many people to a deeper appreciation of the great scriptural heritage that is ours.

J.E. Spicer, CSsR
Edmonton

Introduction

How to Use This Resource

Preparing for Sunday is a hands-on, accessible resource for people who wish to explore more deeply the readings for the coming Sunday. Each Sunday lists the readings of the day, offers a brief reflection on the readings and how they relate to our lives today, and ends with four questions.

Begin your reflection time with a prayer. Then read aloud each of the scripture readings listed. After reading my reflection, explore the four questions. If you are part of a group, you may wish to use these "points of departure" to stimulate discussion; if you are using the book on your own, you may simply reflect on the questions or write in a journal. These questions may be reworded or adapted for your setting.

The readings for each Sunday are from the Sunday Lectionary. The Sunday readings are in a three-year cycle (Year A, B and C). Each year begins with the first Sunday of Advent and ends with the feast of Christ the King. You will find the readings in a missal or missalette.

Welcome to *Preparing for Sunday*! May the time you spend reflecting on the Word of God bear much fruit!

First Sunday of Advent

Isaiah 2:1-5
Romans 13:11-14
Matthew 24:37-44

Dangerous Monotony

Constantly repeated sounds can lull us into sleep. The repetitive lapping of waves on the shore, steady raindrops falling on the roof and other such sounds tend to dull our awareness.

On a deeper level the world about us, with its daily demands, has the same effect. It doesn't put us to sleep; rather, more dangerously, it makes us forget the important truths of life. Eventually we find ourselves on the outer edge of our Christian faith. It recedes into the background, with little effect in shaping our lives.

That is why we need Advent. It reminds us forcibly that the things of this world are passing away, while at our doorstep is the stream of eternal life bearing riches and happiness beyond imagining.

I invite you, then, to reflect on the readings for this, the first Sunday of Advent.

In the first reading, the prophet Isaiah shares with us his inspired vision of end-time. Despite the blaring boasts of secular powers sounding from mountain strongholds he sees that in the long run only God will prevail.

> In days to come the mountain of the Lord's house shall be established as the highest of the mountains.... all the nations shall stream

to it...and say, "Come, let us go up to the mountain of the Lord...that he may teach us his ways...." For out of Zion shall go forth instruction.... He shall judge between the nations.... they shall beat their swords into ploughshares.

In the second reading Paul sees Isaiah's vision approaching completion. To the Christians in Rome he writes, "You know what time it is, how it is now the moment for you to wake from sleep. For salvation is nearer to us now than when we became believers.... put on the Lord Jesus Christ."

In the gospel Jesus shouts a warning: "As the days of Noah were, so will be the coming of the Son of Man." Everyone laughed as Noah built the ark. Likewise, the worldly-wise today give us a pitying laugh as we go about announcing God's reign. But we hear again these words of Jesus: "Therefore you also must be ready, for the Son of Man is coming at an unexpected hour."

The choice is ours. We can let ourselves be lulled by the dull, monotonous sounds of the marketplace or we can sit up, take notice, and follow the way of Christ.

❦

1. How does day-to-day living dull your awareness of your faith?
2. How does worldliness rob Christian faith?
3. How do you react to the truth of end-time?
4. What word or phrase from the readings will you carry with you this week?

Second Sunday of Advent

Isaiah 11:1-10
Romans 15:4-9
Matthew 3:1-12

Not Gloom, nor Doom, but Boom

If we look upon the world scene today through the eyes of the media, we can only be pessimistic about the future. Terrorism abounds. Pollution is destroying our atmosphere, our trees and our waters. The ozone layer, which protects us from the sun's harmful rays, is weakening. Nations are collapsing under great debts. And the list goes on.

Thank heavens there is another side to this gloomy scenario. It comes through in the readings for this second Sunday of Advent.

Looking out on the world of his day, Isaiah sees nothing but political disaster on every front. Despite this he knows that God will not let the people down. God will send them a leader who will lead them to victory. So he prophesies,

> A shoot shall come out from the stump of Jesse [David's Father].... the spirit of the Lord shall rest on him, the spirit of wisdom and understanding.... The spirit of knowledge and the fear of the Lord.... He shall not judge by what his eyes see...but with righteousness he shall judge the poor.

Not only does Isaiah foresee such a leader emerging from the Davidic line, he also foresees that under him a great and final victory will be gained. There will surely come an era of peace when the wolf and the lamb will live together, when the whole country will be filled with the knowledge of the Lord, and "On that day the root of Jesse shall stand as a signal to the peoples; the nations shall inquire of him, and his dwelling shall be glorious."

In the second reading Paul also sounds a note of hope. He clearly states, "Whatever was written in former days was written for our instruction, so that by steadfastness and by the encouragement of the scriptures we might have hope."

In the gospel, John the Baptist heralds the coming of that leader whom Isaiah promised. He proclaims, "Repent, for the kingdom of heaven has come near." In other words, God is about to fulfill the promise of salvation to all peoples.

When the Pharisees and Sadducees came to him out of curiosity, but with no intention of believing him, John upbraids them and warns them of the coming judgment. Then he says to all his listeners: "One who is more powerful than I is coming after me: I am not worthy to carry his sandals. He will baptize you with the Holy Spirit and fire."

So there we have it. A solid assurance of hope given us in the Old Testament and fulfilled in Christ. No matter how bleak the prevailing view of our future, we need not despair. It is not the media that ultimately determine the future. God does. And God makes it clear that the future will far exceed our greatest expectations. Freed from gloom, we are better able to respond to the challenge of the kingdom, thus moving our world to its true destiny.

1. How do the media affect and colour your life?
2. Do you think Isaiah's expectations of a better world to come were too hopeful?
3. John the Baptist said that Jesus will baptize with the Holy Spirit and fire. How do you feel the presence of the Holy Spirit and of fire in you?
4. What word or phrase from the readings will you carry with you this week?

Third Sunday of Advent

Isaiah 35:1-6a, 10
James 5:7-10
Matthew 11:2-11

"Courage! Do Not Be Afraid!"

Most of our fears stem from the unknown. In the middle of the night we hear a noise. If we can identify it, we go back to sleep; otherwise, we begin to worry. When our car engine develops a strange sound, we fear that unless we do something about it we may be in for an expensive repair job. When we feel unwell, we worry until the doctor assures us that there's nothing seriously wrong.

The future is a great unknown. That is why we have some fear of it. But help is at hand through the readings from this third Sunday of Advent.

In the first reading Isaiah addresses his people, who are very despondent about their immediate future. They are exiled in Babylon. Will their slavery never end? Will it end in annihilation? Isaiah comforts them with strong words: "Strengthen the weak hands, and make firm the feeble knees. Say to those who are of a fearful heart, 'Be strong, do not fear! Here is your God.... He will come and save you.'" Isaiah then promises that the time is coming when the blind will see, the deaf hear, the lame walk, and the dumb speak.

In the second reading James counsels the people to be patient and not to lose heart for, as he avows, "The coming of the Lord is near."

In the gospel Matthew tells us how John the Baptist sent his followers to ask Jesus, "Are you the one who is to come, or are we to wait for another?" Jesus does not give them a direct answer. Rather, he says to them, "Go and tell John what you hear and see: the blind receive their sight, the lame walk, the lepers are cleansed, the deaf hear, the dead are raised, and the poor have good news brought to them. And blessed is anyone who takes no offence at me."

John and his followers knew the Hebrew scriptures well. They were fully aware of all the promises made by Isaiah and the other prophets. They also recognized that in his reply to them, Jesus clearly implied that he was fulfilling those promises, that indeed he was the long-awaited Messiah.

We are thus in a position to face the future with confidence. Even the thought of dying, as difficult as it is, has been robbed of its sharp edge, for we know that a loving God will take care of us. In death he awaits us with tender arms, eager to share with us unlimited joy.

1. Share your fears of the future.
2. Isaiah's words in the first reading were addressed to the Jews exiled in Babylon. What are some of your own experiences of "being in exile"?
3. How do you see Jesus grounding your hopes for the future?
4. What word or phrase from the readings will you carry with you this week?

Fourth Sunday of Advent

Isaiah 7:10-14
Romans 1:1-7
Matthew 1:18-24

Help!

We cannot become fully human by ourselves. We need the help of other people. More importantly, we need God's help, as we see in the readings for this last Sunday of Advent.

In the first reading, Ahaz, king of Judah, refuses to ask God's help, even though he is in dire need. Rather than seek a sign from the God of Israel that all would turn out well for himself and for his people, he turns to the king of Assyria. Angered by Ahaz's unbelief, Isaiah prophesies that "the young woman is with child and shall bear a son, and shall name him Immanuel" [God with us].

The "young woman" to whom Isaiah referred to is one of king Ahaz's wives (it was customary at that time for kings to have many wives). Thus, despite Ahaz's unbelief, Isaiah knows that God would see to it that a king from the line of Ahaz (and David) would one day save Israel.

In his letter to the Romans, Paul makes clear that Isaiah's promise was fulfilled in Jesus. For Jesus, he writes, "was declared to be Son of God with power...by resurrection from the dead."

In the gospel Matthew also assures us that Isaiah's prophecy was fulfilled – indeed, wonderfully fulfilled. He writes that an angel appeared to

Joseph and said, "Joseph, son of David, do not be afraid to take Mary as your wife, for the child conceived in her is from the Holy Spirit." The angel goes on to say that Mary's child was to be called "Emmanuel" [God with us]. And with this very name Matthew also ends his gospel.

These readings remind us that in relying on God while remaining open to human help, we will indeed navigate the waters of life successfully.

∽◈∾

1. What kinds of help do you receive from other people?
2. How has God helped you in your life?
3. How do such experiences of human and divine assistance help us to live a Christian life?
4. What word or phrase from the readings will you carry with you this week?

Christmas

Isaiah 62:11-12
Titus 3:4-7
Luke 2:15-20

The Gift of Gifts

Think about the Christmas gifts you chose for people this year. How much they cost does not matter. What does matter is that they express your sincere love and devotion. Without such love, your gift means little. With love, the least of your gifts becomes great.

The truth of this insight is made clear by the readings taken from the liturgy for the Christmas Mass at dawn.

In the first reading, Isaiah assures us that God seeks us out. God does so because God loves us – each one of us, without exception.

In his letter to Titus, Paul states that God's gift to us of the Son springs from "the goodness and loving kindness of God." This great gift is given to us not because of any merit of our own. It comes as a pure gift. And God does not give stintingly. As Paul says, "This Spirit God poured out on us richly."

The gospel is a continuation of Luke's words read at the midnight Mass. The shepherds go to Bethlehem to "see this thing that has taken place." They find "Mary and Joseph, and the child lying in the manger." Both Mary and Joseph are amazed at what the shepherds tell them. Luke, through

Mary, gives us a clue as to how we are to react to the mystery in the manger. For Mary "treasured all these words and pondered them in her heart."

Truly the birth of Jesus is the gift of gifts. For God does not give us an object, a thing, but gives us his only Son. Could there be any greater gift?

⌒๑⌒

1. How does genuine love "upgrade" all the gifts beneath the Christmas tree?
2. How is Jesus the "gift of gifts"?
3. The act of receiving a gift is very important. How are we to receive the gift of God's Son?
4. What word or phrase from the readings will you carry with you this week?

Holy Family

Sirach 3:2-6, 12-14
Colossians 3:12-21
Matthew 2:13-15, 19-23

How to Solve a Problem

To solve a problem we first must analyze it.
We look at it from all angles. We uncover as best
we can all the many factors that are involved in
it. Finally, after due consideration, we go about
solving it.

No one will deny that we are facing many
critical problems in our world today. When we
study them, one common factor shows up in
many of them: family life. If family life is strong
and healthy, many of our critical problems can
be solved. If family life is allowed to weaken,
then the critical problems will become crises,
perhaps unsolvable ones.

This Sunday is the feast of the Holy Family,
an opportune time to assess our family life. Is it
healthy or not? The readings chosen for the feast
help us in this quest.

The first reading, from the Book of Sirach,
begins with these words: "The Lord honours a
father above his children, and he confirms a
mother's right over her children. Those who
honour their father atone for sins, and those
who respect their mother are like those who lay
up treasure."

These and the other words of this reading
remind us that parents are to be given love,

respect and obedience, even when old age over-takes them and there may be no one to care for them except their offspring.

In the second reading Paul speaks of the many virtues to be practised by God's people, and encourages husbands and wives to lovingly defer to one another. And, in regard to their children, he says, "Fathers, do not provoke your children, or they may lose heart."

In the gospel Matthew tells of the Holy Family's escape from Herod through the flight into Egypt. Just as Moses led his people out of slavery in Egypt into the promised land, so now Jesus, coming into our slavery through his incarnation, leads us out of our sinful, captive state into true and full liberty in the loving arms of God.

Thus the centre of life, and of Christian family life, is Jesus. To meet our critical problems today, parents must emphasize more than ever that Jesus is central. The Church itself remains important, but Jesus is the life of the Church. Without Jesus the Church has no meaning.

～☙～

1. Name some of the factors in today's world that make a healthy family life difficult to attain.
2. Despite the factors you have named, what steps can you take to restore your family life to a more healthy state?
3. How can families help elderly parents or grandparents?
4. What ideas from the readings for this Sunday can help you strengthen your family life?

Mary, Mother of God (January 1)

Numbers 6:22-27
Galatians 4:4-7
Luke 2:16-21

Mary, Our Model

Have you made any New Year's resolutions? It's a good idea. We can always try to do better, and the beginning of the year is a good time to start.

No need, however, to look far and wide for the most important of resolutions. It's staring us in the face. It's in the gospel for today's feast of Mary, Mother of God.

Luke tells us about Mary's reaction to the shepherds' visit to Bethlehem, when they explained to Joseph and Mary what they had heard from the angel about Jesus' birth. After they departed, "Mary treasured all these words and pondered them in her heart."

There we have it. Like Mary, the first and model disciple of her Son, we too are to treasure the birth of Jesus and ponder it. This is the best of resolutions, for in becoming human in Jesus God tells us much about ourselves.

The other readings for this feast day also help us to understand and live the mystery of the incarnation. In the first reading Aaron blesses his sons: "The Lord bless you and keep you; the Lord make his face shine upon you, and be gracious to you; the Lord lift up his countenance upon you, and give you peace."

In Jesus God blesses us, comforts us, loves us beyond all telling.

In the second reading Paul sums up Jesus' birth in the following words: "When the fullness of time had come, God sent his Son, born of a woman, born under the law, in order to redeem those who were under the law, so that we might receive adoption as children."

Indeed, through Jesus we are children of God. God's life is in us drawing us to the very heart of the triune God.

Incarnation is thus a mystery to ponder deeply and treasure highly. It is a clue to our true identity and ultimate destiny.

Like Mary, then, we are to treasure all these words and "ponder" them. This is the best New Year's resolution we can make.

꧁❀꧂

1. Think of a practical way to keep Jesus' birth in mind throughout the coming year and resolve to do it.
2. God shares his life with us in many and varied ways. How is this true for you?
3. What does it mean to be God's adopted daughters and sons? How does this affect our relationship with this world and with the people of our times?
4. What word or phrase from the readings will you carry with you this week?

Epiphany

Isaiah 60:1-6
Ephesians 3:2-3a, 5-6
Matthew 2:1-12

Shells Are for Turtles

At one time or another, most of us have been tempted to draw back from close relationships. We have been hurt too much. Security, our heart says, is found in a shell.

Such a temptation is understandable, but we must be aware of its danger. To go into a shell and remain there invites tragedy. No one can continue growing while in a shell. That is why the feast of Epiphany is so important. It urges us to be open to God and to one another just as God has opened himself to us.

In the first reading, Isaiah joyfully sings out to the people of Israel:

> Arise, shine, for your light has come and the glory of the Lord has risen upon you.... Lift up your eyes and look around.... the wealth of the nations shall come to you. A multitude of camels shall cover you.... all those from Sheba will come. They shall bring gold and frankincense, and shall proclaim the praise of the Lord.

Isaiah did not live to see his words fulfilled. He knew, however, that God could never remain hidden. Divine light would shine out. That hope sustained him, as indeed it sustained Israel, and now sustains us.

In the second reading, Paul tells his listeners that God no longer belongs solely to Israel. "The gentiles," he says, "have become fellow heirs, members of the same body, and sharers in the promise in Christ Jesus through the gospel."

The seed of God's self-disclosure was first given to Israel. It was nourished in Israel's soil. But it was always meant to enrich the nations. Now it has, through Christ.

The gospel of the Epiphany tells us about the Magi, the wise men from the East who, guided by a star, came to Bethlehem. There "they saw the child with Mary his mother; and they knelt down and paid him homage. Then, opening their treasure chests, they offered him gifts of gold, frankincense and myrrh."

In the crib, having taken on our humanity, God opens himself to us. We in turn are to be open to him. Later on, Christ would experience rejection – by his own people, even by his intimate associates. Yet in death/resurrection he offered himself anew to everyone. This gives us the strength to overcome any tendency to retreat into a shell. Epiphany is truly a feast of "openness."

1. Recall and describe a "shell" experience you have had.
2. Even the Church (both local and universal) can get into a "shell." Can you think of an example?
3. In taking on our human nature, God became accessible to all people. How do you help people (of various faiths) be more open to God?
4. What word or phrase from the readings will you carry with you this week?

Baptism of the Lord

Isaiah 42:1-4, 6-7
Acts 10:34-38
Matthew 3:13-17

Freedom Fighters

Exploitation has been around ever since we humans began to form larger social groups. The more powerful take to themselves the richer lands and the better goods, leaving only left-overs to the weaker. Moreover, the more power-ful set up structures to protect and maintain their wealth, even though such structures make the poor even poorer.

Because of this oppression every age has its freedom fighters – heroic men and women who recognize exploitation for what it is and try to do something about it. Foremost among these fighters are God-inspired prophets of old and, above all, "the prophet" whom God sent to be the ultimate champion of all the exploited: his own Son.

In the readings for this Sunday, the Baptism of the Lord, we hear a lot about freedom fighters.

In the first reading, Isaiah encourages the Jewish exiles in Babylon with these words: "Here is my servant, whom I uphold.... I have put my spirit upon him; he will bring forth justice to the nations.... He will not grow faint or be crushed until he has established justice in the earth."

Isaiah goes on to say that this servant of whom he writes is Israel itself: "I am the Lord, I have called you in righteousness.... I have given you as covenant to the people, a light to the nations, to open the eyes that are blind, to bring out the prisoners from the dungeon, from the prison those who sit in darkness."

The people of God – all of them – are thus chosen to be freedom fighters: not only Israel, but peoples of all nations. In the second reading Peter says, "I truly understand that God shows no partiality, but in every nation anyone who fears him and does what is right is acceptable to him." He adds, "You know the message he sent to the people of Israel, preaching peace by Jesus Christ – he is Lord of all." And Jesus Christ, Peter says, "went about doing good and healing all who were oppressed by the devil, for God was with him."

Evil is, and has always been, the root cause of all exploitation. In Jesus, however, it has more than met its match. For, as the gospel explains, he is the one whom God had promised to send in order to end all exploitation.

Jesus went to John for baptism, thus showing solidarity with the past of Israel. At his baptism, "the heavens were opened to him and he saw the Spirit of God descending like a dove and alighting on him. And a voice from heaven said, 'This is my Son, the Beloved, with whom I am well pleased.'"

We, the followers of Jesus, continue his fight for freedom. Like him, we are sent to seek out and destroy all the forms of exploitation that hold people in bondage: from the healing of hurts caused by the wear and tear of everyday life to the battle against oppressive structures maintained by the powerful of this world. We are called to reach out to help the poor, enabling them to join more fully in the pilgrimage to God as we look forward to attaining the ultimate freedom that only God can give.

1. What kind of exploitation goes on in your community?
2. The first Jewish Christians knew that the "servant" Isaiah had in mind was Israel itself, but they also realized how much more fully Jesus fulfilled the servant role. How is Jesus the "servant" Isaiah describes?
3. How do you see yourself as a "freedom fighter"?
4. What word or phrase from the readings will you carry with you this week?

Second Sunday in Ordinary Time

Isaiah 49:3, 5-6
1 Corinthians 1:1-3
John 1:29-34

"Hey, You! I've Got Work for You!"

How welcome would such a greeting be to
someone out of work! And even if one did have
a job, such a greeting would arouse curiosity.
What work was being offered?

God addresses the above words to each of us.
They may not be phrased so colloquially, or
come to us as a heavenly voice, but that they are
directed to each of us is clear from this Sunday's
readings.

In the first reading the Lord speaks to Israel
in these words: "You are my servant, Israel, in
whom I will be glorified." God will be glorified
as the Israelite exiles return to their homeland
and there worship God more fully. But that isn't
all. "It is too small a thing that you should be my
servant to raise up the tribes of Jacob and to
restore the survivors of Israel; I will give you as a
light to the nations, that my salvation may reach
to the end of the earth."

The early Christians soon came to realize
that Jesus himself was the servant par excellence of whom Isaiah spoke. He came to bring
both Israel and all peoples of the world to ultimate fulfillment.

In the second reading Paul speaks of himself as "an apostle of Christ Jesus." As such he addresses members of the Church in Corinth, all of whom are called, as he said, "to be saints."

In other words, as Christians we, too, are called by God to join with his Son in witnessing to the world about God's truth.

In the gospel John the Baptist points to Jesus as "the Lamb of God who takes away the sin of the world." He likewise attests, "I saw the Spirit descending from heaven like a dove, and it remained on him.... And I myself have seen and have testified that this is the Son of God."

Like John the Baptist, we are called to witness in word and deed that Jesus is indeed the Chosen One of God. In him, and in him alone, can we find ultimate fulfillment. He is the good news – that God loves us despite our unworthiness.

Each Christian, however, is unique. Each will witness to Jesus differently because of his or her particular character and gifts. But all of us together are to be a powerful sign that God is at work in the world.

We are all challenged to be in the service of God. We are challenged to awaken all Christians to an ever-greater awareness of their true dignity, and to alert all those of other faiths and no faith that God loves them and calls them to an everlasting destiny.

❧❀☙

1. How have you experienced a call from God?
2. How is God's call to each of us to be fulfilled within the people of God (the Church)?
3. Jesus is the Chosen One of God, as John the Baptist attests. Reflect on this central truth of our faith.
4. What word or phrase from the readings will you carry with you this week?

Third Sunday in Ordinary Time

Isaiah 9:1-4
1 Corinthians 1:10-13, 17-18
Matthew 4:12-23

Pessimistic? Read on!

There are times in each of our lives when we feel downhearted. Ordinarily we bounce back to a more normal state. Sometimes, however, we become prey to a more prolonged pessimism.

This Sunday's readings are a powerful antidote to such a pessimistic state of mind.

In the first reading, Isaiah addresses the plight of the entire northern tribes of Israel, here represented by Zebulun and Naphtali. They had been overwhelmed by a powerful Assyrian army and their entire territory taken over. They gave up all hope. But Isaiah thinks otherwise: "In the former time the Lord brought into contempt the land of Zebulun and the land of Naphtali, but in the latter time he will make glorious...the land beyond Jordan, Galilee of the nations."

And indeed God did, for Jesus spent most of his public ministry in Galilee. He was indeed a light to "those who lived in a land of deep darkness."

The second reading concerns the deep divisions that arose among the Christians of Corinth. Some were saying, "I belong to Paul," or "I belong to Cephas," or "I belong to Christ." Doesn't this remind you of the many divisions in the Church today? Paul's answer to the Corinthians is also good for us: "Has Christ been divided? Was Paul crucified for you?"

Some of our current divisions are over serious matters. Keeping the unity of Christ's body in mind will enable us to seek solutions in greater peace and charity.

In the gospel Matthew recalls Isaiah's words about Zebulun and Naphtali and recognizes how wonderfully Jesus fulfilled them, for in Galilee Jesus inaugurated his public ministry, announcing that the kingdom of God was near at hand.

Whenever pessimism hits us, we have a sure remedy. As Paul puts it in his letter to the Romans, "We know that all things work together for good for those who love God, who are called according to his purpose" (8:28).

1. Describe an experience where your pessimism turned into joy.
2. What does it mean to be a part of Christ's body?
3. Name one divisive issue in the Church today. In light of being one in Christ, how would you go about settling this issue?
4. What word or phrase from the readings will you carry with you this week?

Fourth Sunday in Ordinary Time

Zephaniah 2:3, 3:12-13
1 Corinthians 1:26-31
Matthew 5:1-12a

Power Is Not the Name of the Game

Behind much of the political and economic life of today is power. To obtain power, people seek out high positions and wealth. Power means financial security. It also means dominance over others. The powerful can use people to serve their own interests.

Power, however, is not the real name of the game! It is a false god, and as such will always betray its worshippers. Life is the process of becoming human, and the name of the game is not power but humility. This truth resounds in the readings for this Sunday.

The first reading is from the prophet Zephaniah. He lived at a time when the northern part of Israel had already fallen to the Assyrians and the southern part was being threatened by the Babylonians.

Zephaniah realized that military might was not the way to true human fulfillment. Might often brings terror and suffering. True fulfillment can only be found in God. Thus Zephaniah counsels his compatriots, "Seek the Lord, all you humble of the land, who do his commands; seek righteousness, seek humility." He concludes that if people follow this advice, "they will pasture and lie down, and no one shall make them afraid."

In the second reading Paul lays it on the line for the Corinthians: "Not many of you were wise by human standards, not many were powerful, not many were of noble birth." He concludes with these words: "God chose what is low and despised in the world, things that are not, to reduce to nothing things that are, so that no one might boast in the presence of God. God is the source of your life in Christ Jesus, who became for us wisdom from God.... Let the one who boasts, boast in the Lord."

The gospel is from Matthew's Sermon on the Mount, the Magna Carta of God's kingdom. He begins with the beatitude "Blessed are the poor in spirit, for theirs is the kingdom of heaven."

The central point of these three readings is clear. To be human is to acknowledge that we are not God but rather from God, that we are wholly dependent on God, and are to obey God. To depend solely on human power is illusory. It will always end up in loss.

The name of the game is thus not power but humility. For only in acknowledging our dependence on God will God be on our side. And, as Paul says, "If God is for us, who is against us?" (Romans 8:31)

1. Describe an experience you have had, or observed, where power led to downfall.
2. Name some humble people you know or have heard about. Why are you attracted to them?
3. How does true humility enhance our gifts and abilities? Why is humility real strength?
4. What word or phrase from the readings will you carry with you this week?

Fifth Sunday in Ordinary Time

Isaiah 58:6-10
1 Corinthians 2:1-5
Matthew 5:13-16

Christ, the Measure of Giving

The poor and disadvantaged are everywhere. They may live next door to us; they certainly live in our community, our country, our world.

What are we to do about the poor and disadvantaged? An easy question to ask, but not so easy to answer, or to practise. This is especially true in our complicated world. Many social and relief agencies are at work in the field, but many power structures prevent the poor and disadvantaged from rising above their lot. What can we do?

The readings for this Sunday may not fully solve this dilemma, but they do set out some guidelines.

The first reading reminds us forcefully that we have a strict obligation to help the poor and disadvantaged. We cannot pass this obligation onto someone else or onto some agency.

In answer to the question about true worship, Isaiah says, "Is it not to share your bread with the hungry, and bring the homeless poor into your house; when you see the naked, to cover them, and not to hide yourself from your own kin?" In accepting these obligations, Isaiah concludes, "Your light shall rise in the darkness and your gloom be like the noonday."

In the second reading Paul points out to the Christians at Corinth, "I did not come proclaiming the mystery of God to you in lofty words or wisdom. For I decided to know nothing among you except Jesus Christ...so that your faith might rest not on human wisdom but on the power of God."

Here we have two important guidelines for fulfilling our obligation to the poor and disadvantaged. First, our goal must not only be to relieve distress and impoverishment, as good as that intention is; our motives must go deeper. We are to see Christ in the poor and disadvantaged. He identified with them. So must we.

Second, Paul says that the measure of our giving is the crucified Christ. He gave up all things, even his very life, to help us. In helping others we must be prepared to go to the same length, scary as that might be.

If we take to heart, and put into practice, the lessons of these two readings, then we'll fulfill the challenge set in the gospel. "You are the salt of the earth," Jesus said to his followers. If that salt loses its flavour, he explained, it becomes worthless. "You are the light of the world." He then said, "Let your light shine before others, so that they may see your good works and give glory to your Father in heaven."

With these readings ringing in our ears, we will stand up and side with the poor and the disadvantaged.

1. What are your concerns for the poor and the disadvantaged? How have you, in practical ways, followed up on your concerns?
2. Today we are used to having government agencies look after the poor. Now that the government is cutting back on this aid, what are we to do?
3. Reflect on Blessed Mother Teresa as a guide to helping the poor.
4. Think of the poor in your own neighbourhood. How can you help them?

Sixth Sunday in Ordinary Time

Sirach 15:15-20
1 Corinthians 2:6-10
Matthew 5:17-37

Religious Education Dropouts

We are living in a sophisticated age. Most young people finish high school, with a good percentage going on to further education in technical schools, community colleges and universities.

Those who make full use of all the educational possibilities today know that their learning is not over when they graduate. It must continue in order for them to stay on top of their particular field of work.

Those who drop out of school do so at their own peril: there are few good job opportunities for people with less education. Religious education dropouts lose out, too. As this Sunday's readings tell us, the wisdom God offers us towers in importance over any learning the world has to offer.

The first reading (written by Sirach, who lived near the beginning of the second century BC) stands as an introduction to God's wisdom: "For great is the wisdom of the Lord; he is mighty in power and sees everything."

This wisdom is within our grasp. God offers it to us. Moreover, God emphasizes that to accept or refuse it is a matter of life or death. The responsibility is ours.

Paul is even more to the point. He writes: "Among the mature we do speak wisdom, though it is not a wisdom of this age or of the rulers of this age.... We speak God's wisdom, secret and hidden." Paul concludes: "These things God has revealed to us through the Spirit."

In the gospel Jesus tells us that he has a new depth of wisdom for us, a wisdom that goes beyond what had been taught: several times he says, "You have heard that it was said to those of ancient times.... But I say to you...." Each time, what Jesus says offers new depth to received wisdom.

If we take these readings seriously, we receive a big jolt! Many of us – indeed, in some way, all of us – have been "dropouts" from the school of God's wisdom. Having once learned our catechism, we thought we knew it all. But who knows God fully? Who completely plumbs the depths of his wisdom? In this Sunday's readings God invites all of us to take up the quest for his wisdom once again. To say "yes" is to choose life.

1. No matter how busy we are, we can find ways to deepen our knowledge of our faith. Name some of these ways.
2. Reflect on Paul's words in his letter to the Corinthians: "We speak God's wisdom, secret and hidden.... These things God has revealed to us through the Spirit; for the Spirit searches everything." What does this mean for you?
3. Stories are a good way to learn. Name a bible story that speaks to you. What does it teach you?
4. What word or phrase from the readings will you carry with you this week?

Seventh Sunday of Ordinary Time

Leviticus 19:1-2, 17-18
1 Corinthians 3:16-23
Matthew 5:38-48

Being What We're Meant to Be

Dad was taking care of his five-year-old son. To keep him busy, he cut up a map of the world and challenged his son to put it together. In no time flat the lad had it done. Astounded, the father asked how he did it so quickly. "Well," the boy said, "on the back of the map was a picture of a man. So I put the man together and the world came into place."

This story contains a valuable reminder for us to put ourselves together as God meant us to be. How do we know what God wants us to be? This Sunday's readings point the way.

The first reading, from the Book of Leviticus, has God instructing Moses to tell the people of Israel, "You shall be holy, for I the Lord your God am holy." What does it mean to be holy? God lists several things we should not do if we are to be holy, and then the essential commandment: we are to love our neighbour as ourselves.

In the second reading Paul reminds us that we are "God's temple," for the Holy Spirit dwells in us. He also reminds us that "the wisdom of this world is foolishness with God."

In the gospel Jesus forthrightly tells us to turn the other cheek, to go the extra mile. He tells us to love our enemies and pray for those who persecute us. The reading ends with a tough challenge: "Be perfect, therefore, as your heavenly Father is perfect."

What a challenge God gives us! But God also gives us a way to meet that challenge, for as St. Paul says, "you belong to Christ, and Christ belongs to God." We can truly become who God wants us to be.

⌒❀⌒

1. What comes to mind when you are asked, "What is holiness?"
2. What does it mean to be God's temple?
3. The gospel is from Jesus' Sermon on the Mount. What impresses you most in this reading?
4. What word or phrase from the readings will you carry with you this week?

Eighth Sunday in Ordinary Time

Isaiah 49:13-15
1 Corinthians 4:1-5
Matthew 6:24-34

Our Whirling World

This world of ours has always been on the move, but never so quickly as now. Under an ever more searching and inventive technology, our speed today is reaching whirlwind proportions. How can we find peace and equilibrium in such a world? This Sunday's readings offer some guidance.

Let us begin with the gospel. By doing so, we can more clearly understand the other two readings.

Jesus puts first things first: "But strive first for the kingdom of God and his righteousness, and all these things will be given to you as well." The kingdom of God is an eternal reality. The kingdoms of this world are not. This "eternal world" of God's kingdom is now in our midst: correcting our vision, strengthening our resolves, and giving us true insight into what life is all about.

Thus our top priority is God's kingdom, God's saving presence in our midst. Only through this presence can we be truly human. And only by being truly human under God can we transform our world into one of peace and justice.

In the second reading Paul points out to his Corinthian converts that we are to be "servants of Christ and stewards of God's mysteries." Paramount amidst these mysteries is the kingdom of God. If we allow this mystery to shape us, we can in turn shape the world.

Does this sound utopian? How can we shape the world? We cannot do it alone, but God is doing it and asks us to do our part. For courage to do our part we turn to the first reading.

"Sing for joy, O heavens, and exult, O earth.... For the Lord has comforted his people and will have compassion on his suffering ones." Though we may be tempted to say that God has forsaken us in our struggles, God reassures us, "Can a woman forget her nursing child, or show no compassion for the child of her womb? Even these may forget, yet I will not forget you."

What comforting words! God will never abandon us. We must work to better our world. But such work, indeed all human work, will be useless unless we are rooted in God's kingdom. Our Christian challenge is thus to stand steady in our whirling world by keeping our eyes and our hearts focussed on God's presence, God's kingdom, in our midst.

1. In what ways has our world today "sped up"? What does this mean in your life?
2. How do God's kingdom and our present world fit together?
3. What can you do to help shape this whirlwind world?
4. What word or phrase from the readings will you carry with you this week?

Ninth Sunday in Ordinary Time

Deuteronomy 10:12-13a, 11:18, 26-28, 32
Romans 1:16-17, 3:20-26, 28
Matthew 7:21-27

Getting Right Down to It

In our human affairs, there is time for reflection and a time for talk: then comes a time for action. We have to get right down to it.

Many of us prefer theory to action. It's easy to theorize; action can be, and often is, messy. But both are necessary. Theory without action leads to a stalemate. And action without theory is dangerous. Dynamite can be useful, but if we don't know how to use it disaster will follow.

The readings for this Sunday push us to action in our Christian lives.

In the first reading Moses says to his people, "So now, O Israel, what does the Lord your God require of you? Only to fear the Lord your God, to walk in all his ways, to love him, to serve the Lord your God with all your heart and with all your soul, and to keep the commandments of the Lord your God."

God is clearly calling us to action, but first, we must learn what God wants of us. This learning is a lifelong affair, for God is always teaching us new depths to older truths. And learning should lead to action, encouraging us to get right down to it.

In the gospel Jesus says to us, "Not everyone who says to me 'Lord, Lord,' will enter the kingdom of heaven, but only the one who does the will of my Father in heaven." He follows up these words by saying, "Everyone then who hears these words of mine and acts on them will be like a wise man who built his house on rock."

Jesus is pointing out the importance of actions that are in line with God's will. Christians are called to listen intently to God's words and then act based on those words.

Does this frighten us? Well it might. But God never demands action without giving us the strength to complete it. That is why Paul in the second reading assures the Christians at Rome, "I am not ashamed of the gospel." The gospel is truth: truth that demands action.

Further on, Paul assures the Roman Christians, many of whom were converts from Judaism, that they were no longer being saved by obedience to the law but rather through faith in Jesus. And faith in Jesus demands that we get right down to living our faith, bolstered by the strength of "Christ-in-us, our hope of glory," as Paul never tires of saying.

1. What does "getting right down to it" mean in your daily life?
2. What does it mean for Christians?
3. How do Paul's words to the Romans strengthen us in our Christian action?
4. What word or phrase from the readings will you carry with you this week?

First Sunday of Lent

Genesis 2:7-9, 16-18, 25; 3:1-7
Romans 5:12-19
Matthew 4:1-11

The Real Success Story

Our hearts are deeply touched when we hear a story about someone's rise from the depths of failure to the heights of success. Of all such stories, by far the most inspiring is that of our own humanity. We have come all the way from tragic failure to miraculous success.

The setting for this human story is given in the first reading for this Sunday. The author of Genesis writes, "The Lord God formed man from the dust of the ground, and breathed into his nostrils the breath of life; and the man became a living being." All was unalloyed happiness – perhaps only the happiness of human infancy, but happiness nevertheless.

Then came the tragedy. In the mysterious process of growing towards God, selfishness took over. We gave up on our humanity and chose to be God. This was our tragic error.

Looking back on human history, Paul voices his views on this tragedy. "Just as sin came into the world through one man, and death came through sin, so death spread to all, because all have sinned."

The name of the human tragedy is thus "sin." Fundamentally, sin is a breakdown of that life-imparting relationship that God established with us. Once this break took place it continued to grow worse, threatening an utter and final death. But for God's graciousness, such would certainly have been our terrible ending.

Paul explains to the Romans how God averted this disaster. "For if the many died through the one man's trespass, much more surely have the grace of God and the free gift in the grace of the one man, Jesus Christ, abounded for the many." In other words, Jesus restored us to a right relationship to God, to one another and to our world.

In the gospel we hear about Christ's dramatic conflict with evil. Like Israel of old, Jesus was led into the wilderness. There, for forty days, he was tempted. Unlike Israel, and unlike Adam, Jesus did not succumb to the wiles of evil. Thrice was he tempted and thrice he conquered. "Away with you, Satan!" he finally ordered. "Worship the Lord your God, and serve only him."

What better way to begin our Lenten journey than by reflecting on the meaning of sin as given us in today's readings?

⌇❀⌇

1. Reflect on the tragic fall of humanity, who sinned in wanting to become God.
2. How do you see Jesus as one who reverses the tidal wave of humanity's sinfulness?
3. Jesus banishes Satan and wins the victory over him through his death/resurrection. But evil is still around. What are we to do?
4. What will you do this Lent to strengthen your relationship with God?

Second Sunday of Lent

Genesis 12:1-4
2 Timothy 1:8b-10
Matthew 17:1-9

Needed – Interior Direction

Have you ever been lost in the woods? Or in a big city? In either case, it is not a pleasant experience.

What about those who have lost their spiritual way? They, too, are bewildered and are searching for a way out. This Sunday's readings offer guidance on this issue.

"Go from your country and your kindred and your father's house," God says to Abram, "to the land that I will show you. I will make of you a great nation, and I will bless you, and make your name great, so that you will be a blessing." These lines from the book of Genesis explain how God chose to give direction to humanity. And Abram followed his directions. We are grateful to him. By his decision he took a major step in the way of salvation.

In the second reading Paul says to Timothy, "Join with me in suffering for the gospel, relying on the power of God, who saved us and called us with a holy calling, not according to our works but according to his own purpose and grace." He then goes on to say, "Christ Jesus...abolished death and brought life and immortality to light through the gospel."

The good news Paul speaks of is that Jesus journeyed through life, suffering and death into a new and immortal existence with God. He opened the way for us to do the same, empowering us through the Spirit, who works through the whole people of God.

The gospel tells us about the transfiguration. Underlying the account is the truth that Jesus, in a moment of deep prayer wherein he sought the direction he was to take, decided that it was his Father's will that he go to Jerusalem even though certain death awaited him there. This was a momentous decision. It fulfilled the Law of the chosen people (as symbolized by the presence of Moses) as well as the entire prophetic tradition (as symbolized by Elijah). More than this, it was a decision that was to shape the future. This is clear from what God says to the apostles who witnessed the transfiguration, and to all of us: "This is my Son, the Beloved; with him I am well pleased; listen to him."

Our life-direction as Christians is clear. We are, like Jesus, to set our face towards Jerusalem, the heavenly one. We must be intent on fulfilling God's will, which always entails some type of death-to-self. We are strengthened in knowing that our reward is new life.

In Jesus we have interior direction of the highest possible calibre; what's more, Jesus himself is with us through the Spirit.

1. Describe an experience you've had of being lost (in real life or in a dream).
2. Long before Neil Armstrong walked on the moon, Abram (later Abraham) took a giant step for humankind. Reflect on Abram's momentous act.
3. How is Jesus the ultimate fulfillment of Abraham's step?
4. Name a time when you made a prayerful decision to go a certain way and later discovered what a blessing that decision was.

Third Sunday of Lent

Exodus 17:3-7
Romans 5:1-2, 5-8
John 4:5-42

Our Ultimate RRSP

In our world today, "security" is a fashion-
able word. It is found in many advertisements
and is on the lips of most working people. We all
are looking for security. This is not new, of
course: it was always so. Our cave-dwelling
ancestors sought it, and all future humans will
also seek it.

But what exactly is "security"? This Sunday's
readings point to an answer.

In the first reading the Jewish people, newly
escaped from Egypt, complain of their hard lot
in the desert of Sinai. They say to Moses, "Why
did you bring us out of Egypt?"

Egypt had at least afforded the Jews some
security, though little freedom. Now, in the Sinai
desert, they had freedom but little security. There
was the God of their ancestors, yes, but as they
said to Moses, "Is the Lord among us or not?"

God then commands Moses to take the same
staff that was used to free them from slavery in
Egypt and strike the rock with it. From this rock
life-giving water gushes forth. God is indeed in
their midst.

In the second reading Paul goes right to the
heart of true security: "We have peace with God
through our Lord Jesus Christ.... And hope does

not disappoint us, because God's love has been poured into our hearts through the Holy Spirit that has been given to us."

The gospel describes how a Samaritan woman went to draw water from the village well. She sees Jesus sitting beside it. He asks her for a drink. She wonders why he should speak to her since Jews and Samaritans were traditional enemies. Jesus then says to her, "If you knew the gift of God, and who it is that is saying to you, 'Give me a drink,' you would have asked him, and he would have given you living water."

And what wonderful water Jesus gives! "Those who drink of the water that I will give them will never be thirsty. The water that I will give will become in them a spring gushing up to eternal life."

God, then, is our basic security: a security that brings us to true human fulfillment. And God within us, through the Son and Spirit, is our guarantee of fulfillment and security. God's presence within becomes a fountain springing upward to fullness of life. This is the only ultimately fulfilling security, for it alone is eternal and fully satisfies our deepest longings.

1. In his book *Roots,* Alex Haley quotes his grandmother as saying, "God may not come when you want. But he'll always be there on time." Reflect on this saying. Describe a personal experience where this was the case.

2. Recently I heard a story of a businessman from England who had made a fortune, and who said to the seminarian visiting him that all his wealth meant nothing to him as he faced death. Reflect on this true experience.

3. How does Jesus bring us ultimate security?

4. What word or phrase from the readings will you carry with you this week?

Fourth Sunday of Lent

1 Samuel 16:1b, 6-7, 10-13a
Ephesians 5:8-14
John 9:1-41

True Greatness

Too often we judge people's worth by worldly standards. Have they made it in business, in sports, in the arts? Are they well off? Are they attractive? Do they come from the upper strata of society?

These are false standards for judging real worth. The true standard is given us in the readings for this Fourth Sunday of Lent.

In the first reading Samuel is sent by the Lord to the house of Jesse to choose a king from among his sons. On seeing the eldest of Jesse's sons, Samuel says to himself that he must be the one. But the Lord says to Samuel, "Do not look upon his appearance or on the height of his stature, because I have rejected him; for the Lord does not see as mortals see; they look on the outward appearance, but the Lord looks on the heart."

One after another, the sons of Jesse are presented to Samuel. But Samuel says to Jesse, "The Lord has not chosen any of these. Are all your sons here?" Jesse answers that there is still one left, the youngest. He is looking after the sheep. "Send and bring him," says Samuel. Upon his appearance the Lord says, "Rise and anoint him; for this is the one."

No one thought that the youngest son, David, was capable of being king. But God did.

In the second reading Paul points out to the Ephesians: "Once you were darkness, but now in the Lord you are light."

Many of the chosen people, led by the Pharisees, rejected Jesus. From the middle of the first century on, however, Gentiles were flocking into the Christian community. God's choice settled on those in darkness, not on those who believed themselves to be in the light.

The gospel, a key story in John, describes a controversy between the Pharisees and a man who was born blind but whose sight Jesus restored. In the course of the dialogue it becomes clear that the Pharisees are becoming more blind and obdurate, whereas the cured blind man grows steadily more enlightened and more sure of who Jesus really is, finally saying, "Lord, I believe."

True greatness is thus a gift from God and not a right by birth or by human achievement. For this reason the truly great are always truly humble. They respect and are grateful for their natural talents, but at the same time acknowledge that all true greatness consists in being loved and accepted by God. This greatness is offered to all.

1. Describe an experience you have had of judging others superficially, or being judged that way.
2. The Lord "looks on the heart," as the first reading attests. In looking into another's heart, what qualities that lead to greatness do you look for?
3. In the gospel, how were the Pharisees becoming more blind? How was the blind man starting to see more clearly?
4. What word or phrase from the readings will you carry with you this week?

Fifth Sunday of Lent

Ezekiel 37:12-14
Romans 8:8-11
John 11:1-45

A Way Out

Are you discouraged, worried, uncertain, in pain, oppressed, lonely, forgotten? If so, this Sunday's readings are for you. All three readings challenge us to look up from our despair to a new life and a new hope.

The first reading is from Ezekiel, one of the three prophets who concerned themselves with the Jewish exile in Babylon (modern-day Iraq). He addresses his people who were terribly down-hearted over the loss of their temple, their city (Jerusalem) and their country. Little was left to them. To these down-and-out people Ezekiel, in God's name, says, "I am going to open your graves, and bring you up from your graves, O my people; and I will bring you back to the land of Israel…. I will put my spirit within you, and you shall live."

In Babylon the Jewish people were experiencing a condition similar to their slavery in Egypt 700 years before: their spirits were at their lowest ebb. Ezekiel's words come to them like a shot of adrenaline. As hopeless as things look, Ezekiel assures them, God has not forgotten them. Indeed God has plans for them to return to their own land.

The second reading deals with an even more dreadful and more encompassing exile than that of Babylon. Paul addresses humanity's exile in the "body" – that is, an exile from God characterized by an acceptance of worldly values and standards that are anything but godly.

Paul lifts up the spirits of the Roman Christians with these words:

> Anyone who does not have the Spirit of Christ does not belong to him. But if Christ is in you, though the body is dead because of sin, the Spirit is life because of righteousness. If the Spirit of God who raised Jesus from the dead dwells in you, he who raised Christ from the dead will give life to your mortal bodies also through his Spirit that dwells in you.

What Paul, in his letter to the Romans, says in abstract terms, John, in the gospel, says in concrete terms. Lazarus, Jesus' friend, was seriously ill. His sisters, Martha and Mary, sent word to Jesus about their brother. Jesus delayed coming to them until Lazarus had been dead for four days. Martha's first words to Jesus are, "Lord, if you had been here, my brother would not have died. But even now I know that God will give you whatever you ask of him."

Jesus assures Martha that Lazarus "will rise again." Martha agrees that indeed he will rise again "in the resurrection on the last day." Jesus replies, "I am the resurrection." Martha believes him but does not comprehend what he means until he calls Lazarus forth from the grave with the words "Lazarus, come out!"

Jesus likewise calls each of us out of every twist of fortune that renders us imprisoned and without hope. He is resurrection both on the last day and on every day of our lives.

1. Describe an experience of being disheartened or abandoned.
2. Reflect on Paul's words, "Those who are in the flesh cannot please God." How does Paul point a way out of the flesh?
3. What does Jesus' resurrection mean to you?
4. What word or phrase from the readings will you carry with you this week?

Passion Sunday

Isaiah 50:4-7
Philippians 2:6-11
Matthew 26:14–27:66

A Tough Road to Success

Let's face it. The world today encourages selfishness. It always has, but now more than ever. There is great pressure on those in business, politics, sports, science and the arts to be number one. If they succeed, the world applauds; if they do not, they are ignored. Likewise there is great pressure on everyone to possess more and more consumer goods. The more we own, the higher our status. These are direct and powerful motivations to selfishness.

What are we to do? We have to recognize the superficiality of worldly standards of success. To do so, however, we need clear insight into what constitutes true success. Strange as it may seem, true success is to be found in what the world considers failure, as we see in the readings for Passion Sunday.

The first reading is from one of the four "servant songs" in the book of Isaiah. In these songs Isaiah pictures the true role of Israel as one of redemptive suffering. "I was not rebellious," the servant says. "I did not turn backward. I gave my back to those who struck me, and my cheeks to those who pulled out the beard.... The Lord God helps me; therefore I have not been disgraced."

The "suffering servant" (Israel) is meant to conquer evil not by force but by loving patience under suffering, confident that in the end God will bring about success. The first Christians recognized that in Jesus the servant songs of Isaiah were fulfilled.

In the second reading Paul uses an early Christian hymn to help the Philippians understand the truth about success. Jesus was made in the image of God (like Adam and all human beings), but unlike Adam and us, Jesus "did not regard equality with God as something to be exploited, but emptied himself, taking the form of a slave.... He humbled himself and became obedient to the point of death, even death on a cross." And for this, "God highly exalted him and gave him the name that is above every name."

The gospel, from the passion narrative in the gospel of Matthew, tells us how Jesus accepted death on a cross. Jesus clearly teaches us through his passion that true success comes from emptying ourselves of all pretensions to worldly greatness and devoting our lives to bringing about God's plan of love and justice for all humanity. Such high devotion causes consternation to the vested interests of this world. They oppose it, even to the point of inflicting suffering and death on those who support God's plan.

But neither suffering nor death can thwart God's purpose. Indeed, they become the very stuff of victory. They lead people to God as nothing else would. True success, then, comes from a type of failure – foolishness indeed to the world, but wisdom in the eyes of God.

1. Describe an experience of being "number one."
2. How do you react to worldly standards of success?
3. Reflect on the hymn Paul quotes in the second reading.
4. How is the cross an ultimate failure in a worldly sense, but an ultimate success in the eyes of God and for Christ's followers?

The Triduum

The "Great Sunday"

This little book offers meditations on the Sunday Lectionary readings, and well it should, for Sunday is the original Christian feast day. From the very beginnings of the faith, Christians celebrated Eucharist on the first day of the week (as reckoned according to the Jewish calendar). Why? Sunday marked for them, as it continues to do for us, the first day of the New Creation inaugurated by Christ's resurrection from the dead. By the middle of the second century, Christians began to celebrate with special solemnity the Sunday closest to the Jewish Passover, the time of year that gives the name "paschal" to the saving mystery of Christ's death and resurrection. Quite naturally, this annual Sunday celebration at Passover time was extended to include commemorations of his last supper and his crucifixion, the dramatic events of his last days. This is the origin of the Easter Triduum, the sacred days marking "the culmination of the entire liturgical year" (*General Norms for the Liturgical Year and Calendar*, § 18).

The Easter Triduum, as its name (from Latin) indicates, comprises three days as reckoned according to ancient Jewish custom – a day was measured from sundown to sundown.

Thus, the first day of the triduum commemorates his last supper (Holy Thursday evening) and his crucifixion, death, and burial (Good

Friday afternoon). There are no major liturgical celebrations on the second day (from sundown on Good Friday until sundown on Holy Saturday), for it is a period evoking the time Jesus' body rested in the tomb. The third day, the day on which Jesus rose from the dead, begins at sundown Saturday. This is the evening of the great Easter Vigil, which Saint Augustine once called the "mother of all vigils."

On these three most holy days the Church celebrates its most splendid and awe-inspiring liturgies. The Mass of the Lord's Supper on Thursday evening celebrates Jesus' last meal with his disciples when he blessed the bread and wine with the sacred words so familiar to us. This liturgy also features the ritual washing of the feet as enjoined by Jesus in John 13, and ends with the solemn procession and prayer before the reserve Eucharist at a specially designated repository. The afternoon Celebration of the Lord's Passion marks the highlight of Good Friday when the Passion according to John is solemnly proclaimed, followed by special intercessory prayers for all people, the veneration of the cross, and communion. Originally celebrated from sundown on Holy Saturday evening through dawn on Easter Sunday morning, the vigil comprises the blessing of the new light and the solemn proclamation of Christ's resurrection, extensive readings from the scriptures evoking the story of salvation, the initiation of new candidates in baptism and confirmation, and culminates in the Eucharist. Easter Sunday is in essence but a continuation of this most wonderful celebration.

Anyone wishing to savour the full meaning of what each Sunday celebrates cannot miss participating in the Easter Triduum, for it is, quite simply, SUNDAY writ large.

Professor Normand Bonneau, OMI
Faculty of Theology
Saint Paul University, Ottawa

Easter Sunday

Acts 10:34a, 36-43
Colossians 3:1-4 or 1 Corinthians 5:6b-8
John 20:1-18

The Joy and the Challenge

Easter is the height of our religious celebrations because it represents the ultimate breakthrough – from death to new life. No such breakthrough had ever occurred before. Now it has. Jesus has risen from the dead.

In Easter light, and in that light alone, the shadows and darkness of life receive new meaning. They become part of the breakthrough to new life, just as the pains of childbirth do. Moments of joy and happiness likewise take on newness, for in Easter light they foreshadow the unspeakable joy and happiness still to come.

Easter also assures us that we will find the strength we need to follow Christ through life and through death into resurrection. As Paul puts it, God "gives us the victory through our Lord Jesus Christ" (1 Corinthians 15:57).

Easter is thus a huge sigh of relief to us earthly travellers. It is also a challenge. In its light and strength we are to view life anew, to live it with new purpose, to share it with more zeal.

As you renew your baptismal vows this Easter Sunday, do so with clear mind and full heart, for in Christ we can overcome evil in ourselves and in the world.

In Christ, we are also gifted with a faith that helps us shape this life, and will take us, finally, into the fullness of God's loving embrace.

To all a joyful, challenging Easter!

1. Describe a time when hard work, and even suffering, have led to great joy in your life.
2. Reflect on Paul's words, "Set your minds on things that are above, not on things that are on earth" (Colossians 3:2).
3. Our baptismal promises commit us to overcoming evil and to a deepening faith in God. How can you put these promises into action?
4. What word or phrase from the readings will you carry with you this week?

Second Sunday of Easter

Acts 2:42-47
1 Peter 1:3-9
John 20:19-31

Easter Needs a Follow-up

Important happenings need a follow-up. Their greatness is too rich and too overwhelming for us to absorb all at once. Time and reflection are needed to sound their depth.

This applies to Easter above all. Christ's resurrection was the most dramatic and life-changing event ever. Its profound implications dawned upon Christians only by degrees. Some of these implications emerge in the readings for this second Sunday of the Easter season.

In the first reading, from the Acts of the Apostles, Luke pictures the deep community spirit that flowed from the Easter event. "They devoted themselves to the apostles' teaching and fellowship, to the breaking of bread and the prayers."

Because of the presence of the risen Christ in their midst, a deep bond was forming among his followers. They drew closer to one another as they accepted and practiced the truths handed down to them by the apostles. They gladly shared their food as well as their goods when the need arose.

In the second reading Peter writes to the new Christian communities springing up everywhere, encouraging them to live out their new-found faith. He promises "an inheritance that is imperishable, undefiled, and unfading, kept in heaven for you."

The faithful will have "to suffer various trials," Peter says, but their joy will not diminish, for it is "more precious than gold." Moreover, it will "result in praise and glory and honour when Jesus Christ is revealed."

Thus it was that the first Christians came to understand that the resurrection did not do away with the crosses and trials of life. It did, however, shed a new light on them.

In the gospel John tells how Jesus appeared to the apostles on the first Easter Sunday saying to them, "Peace be with you. As the Father has sent me, so I send you.... Receive the Holy Spirit."

The risen Jesus makes clear that because of his resurrection his followers, empowered by the Spirit, were to go out to the world bearing the good news.

Thomas, one of the Twelve, wasn't present at Jesus' appearance to the others. On hearing of it he doubted that it happened.

Most early Christians had not seen the risen Christ. They were in much the same position as we are. So John uses the story of Thomas to assure them and us that Jesus indeed is truly risen. Jesus says to them, and to us, "Blessed are those who have not seen and yet have come to believe."

Thus Easter is the richest possible resource for reflection on what human life is all about. If we respond to it, it can change our lives as radically as it did the lives of the first Christians.

1. Reflect on a meaningful event in your life and how you realized its depth and richness only long after it happened.
2. Why is the Easter event so meaningful?
3. How do we get back to, and imitate, the first Christian communities as outlined in the reading from Acts?
4. What is your reaction to Thomas' doubts?

Third Sunday of Easter

Acts 2:14, 22b-28
1 Peter 1:17-21
Luke 24:13-35

Surprise!

Interpersonal relationships are never simple. We humans are complex. Our personalities are many-sided. Our relationships, as a result, are always full of surprises.

Our relationship with the risen Christ is full of surprises, too, as we see in this Sunday's readings.

In the first reading Peter addresses an audience of Jews in and around Jerusalem. He accuses them of rejecting Jesus even though Jesus was "a man attested to you by God with deeds of power, wonders, and signs that God did through him among you, as you yourselves know." Peter then explains to his audience that Jesus was indeed their long-awaited Messiah. He quotes the words of Psalm 16: "I saw the Lord always before me...therefore my heart was glad.... For you will not abandon my soul to Hades, or let your Holy One experience corruption."

In the second reading Peter reminds his fellow Christians that they are in a time of exile; that is, they (and all of us) are pilgrims. We are all on the way to God. To travel steadily and well we must always keep in mind the ransom Jesus paid for us. And, we must expect some surprising twists and turns along the way.

The gospel, too, contains a surprise. Two disciples of Jesus were on their way to Emmaus after the shattering experience of the cross. A stranger joined them. They told him about their dashed hopes concerning Jesus. They admitted that some of the women of their group had gone to the tomb where Jesus was placed and found it empty. There, angels told them that Jesus was alive and well, but this did not restore the faith of the disciples, because they did not see him.

The stranger then upbraided them: "Oh, how foolish you are, and how slow of heart to believe all that the prophets have declared! Was it not necessary that the Messiah should suffer these things and then enter into his glory?"

On reaching home the two disciples recognized Jesus as he blessed and broke bread with them. They were astounded, and even more so when he disappeared. Hastily they headed back to Jerusalem to tell the others about their experience. Upon arriving there they found that Jesus had already appeared to the Eleven.

Faith in Jesus is a many-sided relationship. To be in relationship with Jesus is to be in relationship with all things good – past and present, and to come. We are constantly and pleasantly surprised by Jesus, just as the disciples of Emmaus were. Jesus possesses the fullness of risen life, which overflows into our lives in many wonderful and unexpected ways.

1. Describe some of the surprises you have experienced in your relationships.
2. Many of the Jews were not ready to be surprised by the Messiah. They had their own ideas of what a Messiah should be. Reflect on how we can be trapped by our ideas on how the followers of Jesus should act.
3. As pilgrims, how can we take initiative on our journey to God?
4. What word or phrase from the readings will you carry with you this week?

Fourth Sunday of Easter

Acts 2:14a, 36b-41
1 Peter 2:20b-25
John 10:1-10

Living It Up

"Living it up" is a catchphrase that covers many different ways of living. It may refer to squandering money on useless things, it may point to living "high on the hog," or it may simply mean having a great time. In any case we all wish we could live it up a bit more often!

Well, we can. But in a very unexpected way, as the readings for this fourth Sunday in the Easter season explain.

Just after the first followers of Christ experienced the coming of the Spirit at Pentecost, Peter stood up and addressed the crowd that had gathered to find out what the excitement was all about. He boldly says, "Let the entire house of Israel know with certainty that God has made him both Lord and Messiah, this Jesus whom you crucified."

On hearing these words, the gathered people "were cut to the heart." They ask what is expected of them. Peter answers, "Repent, and be baptized every one of you in the name of Jesus Christ so that your sins may be forgiven; and you will receive the gift of the Holy Spirit."

There we have it in a nutshell. To really live it up we must live by the new life Christ offers. It is ours through baptism. Once we are joined to him and to the community of his followers, through baptism our sins are forgiven and the Holy Spirit is given to us. The slate is wiped clean and new life is imparted. High life indeed!

However, as the second reading tells us, this new life isn't all smiles and chuckles. It can bring jealousy and persecution in its wake. Those who do not have new life and whose lifestyle is threatened by it react against it, often violently. Peter explains, "Christ also suffered for you, leaving you an example, so that you should follow in his steps.... When he was abused, he did not return abuse; when he suffered, he did not threaten; but he entrusted himself to the one who judges justly." Christ did this "so that, free from sins, we might live for righteousness."

Our work is cut out for us. The new life we are gifted with has its responsibilities. In receiving, we take all that comes with it.

In the gospel Jesus explains his role as the Risen One by way of a parable. "I am the gate," he teaches. "Whoever enters by me will be saved, and will come in and go out and find pasture." He concludes, "I came that they may have life, and have it abundantly."

Thus there is only one sure way of "living it up" – the way of Jesus. All other ways will prove to be deceptive and short-lived. They may bring temporary distraction but certainly no lasting satisfaction. Jesus alone can give life to the full. Indeed, he himself is the way to a full life. In accepting him, and in giving ourselves wholly to him, we'll reach the heights of living it up.

1. Reflect on your desire to "live it up."
2. How does your new life, received in baptism, help you reframe this desire?
3. Recall a time when you or someone you know suffered because of your faith in Jesus?
4. How is Jesus a gate to good pasture and the giver of abundant life?

Fifth Sunday of Easter

Acts 6:1-7
1 Peter 2:4-9
John 14:1-12

Blossoming Ministries

In the Church of today a great variety of lay ministries is blossoming. This is as it should be. All Christians through baptism join with the risen Jesus and possess the dignity and the responsibility arising from this intimacy.

In order to encourage such a reawakening of ministries, to nurture the fervour and dedication of participants, and to recognize the value of these ministries, it is well to reflect on their foundation in scripture. This Sunday's readings speak out on this very matter.

The first reading tells how the Twelve called a meeting of the first Christian community in order to face new issues arising in their midst. The Twelve made it clear that they could not fulfill all roles themselves. "Therefore, friends, select from among yourselves seven men of good standing, full of the Spirit and of wisdom, whom we may appoint to this task, while we...devote ourselves to prayer and to serving the word."

New ages, such as our own, have needs that previous ones did not know. New needs in turn call for new ministries. The next two readings concentrate on the solid foundation upon which lay ministries are built. Peter, in the second reading, points out how Jesus is "a living stone, though rejected by mortals yet chosen and precious in God's sight.... Like living stones, let yourselves be built into a spiritual house, to be a holy priesthood, to offer spiritual sacrifices acceptable to God through Jesus Christ."

Through baptism all Christians belong to this holy priesthood – "the priesthood of all the faithful." This is the highest honour of being Christian. The laity with their diverse gifts help to further Christ's work on earth.

Lest the dignity of the priesthood of the faithful overawe us, John reminds us in the gospel of these words of Jesus: "Do not let your hearts be troubled. Believe in God, believe also in me.... I am the way and the truth, and the life.... The words that I say to you I do not speak on my own; but the Father who dwells in me does his works."

The Father lives in Jesus, and in us. Therefore, as Jesus says in this Sunday's gospel, "The one who believes in me will also do the works that I do and, in fact, will do greater works than these, because I am going to the Father." We can do even greater works because the Risen Jesus is with us.

Thus the new ministries have solid backing. From the beginning of Christianity they were exercised. Only later were many of the ministries reserved for the clergy at a time when clergy were the only ones with an education. Times have changed. Laity are once again being challenged anew to take a role in ministry, and are reminded that Christ is with them. May the new blossoming of ministries continue and become more widespread!

~⚘~

1. Name some areas where lay people are working in ministry. How are they enriching the life of the Church?

2. The "priesthood of all the faithful" has always been recognized but was downplayed for many centuries. How do you see this priesthood in relation to the Eucharist and to the many ministries the laity today are challenged to exercise?

3. In the gospel Jesus gives solid encouragement to his followers in their ministry. Reflect on Jesus' words in verse 12 and what they mean in your life.

4. What word or phrase from the readings will you carry with you this week?

Sixth Sunday of Easter

Acts 8:5-8, 14-17
1 Peter 3:15-18
John 14:15-21

It's the Spirit that Counts

At times our spirit is down; at other times it is up. When it's down, we see the world and ourselves with jaundiced eyes. Nothing seems right. Nothing goes right. Life isn't worthwhile.

When our spirit is up, the opposite happens. We see the world and ourselves with rose-coloured glasses. Everything seems okay. Everything is going well. Life is worthwhile.

Were we to stay down, goodness knows what would happen. Surely we would be opening ourselves to many ills. Our challenge, then, is to keep our spirits up.

For our spirits to be up, and stay there, God has given us his own Spirit. This we learn from the readings of this sixth Sunday of the Easter season.

The first reading tells us how Philip the apostle took the good news beyond the city of Jerusalem. He journeyed to Samaria and there "proclaimed the Messiah to them" with the result that "unclean spirits, crying with loud shrieks, came out of many who were possessed; and many others who were paralyzed or lame were cured." Word of this success came back to the apostles in Jerusalem, who "sent Peter and

John to them.... [They] laid their hands on them, and they received the Holy Spirit."

With the acceptance of the good news comes a new strength: the strength of the Spirit.

In the second reading Peter begins by telling his readers not to fear, but "in your hearts sanctify Christ as Lord. Always be ready to make your defence to anyone who demands from you an accounting for the hope that is in you." Then he reminds them that sufferings may come upon them. If so they are not to be disheartened, for Christ himself suffered: "He was put to death in the flesh, but made alive in the spirit."

While in the body Christ was still on his journey to God. Sufferings were part of that journey. "In the spirit," however, he was raised up, and "in the spirit" he shares his risen life with us.

In the gospel Jesus promises "another Advocate...the Spirit of truth," who will take up his dwelling within us. We are not left as orphans. Jesus remains with us, and within us, through the Spirit.

How are we to regard the Spirit? Just as we regard Jesus. Just as we know the Father only through Jesus, so do we know the Spirit only through Jesus. The Spirit, coming from the Father and Son, leads us into the dynamism of the Trinity.

Recall these readings, then, when you are feeling down. The Spirit will raise you up!

⌒❀⌒

1. Describe some of your experiences of being "down" in spirit, and being "up" in spirit.
2. Philip dared to leave Jerusalem in order to speak to the Samaritans (with great results!). What does this teach us?
3. In the second reading Peter tells us to be on our toes in defence of the faith. Reflect on his words.
4. What is your understanding and experience of the Spirit in our midst?

Ascension of the Lord

Acts 1:1-11
Ephesians 1:17-23
Matthew 28:16-20

The Ball Is in Our Court

There are times when we, as individuals or as a group, must take action. All the preparation has been done. Now it's up to us.

A teacher, for instance, has taught all that he or she knows about a particular subject. When examination day arrives, students must write the exam. No one else can do it in their place.

This is what Ascension Day is all about. Jesus, in both his earthly and risen life, has done everything possible to fit and train his followers to carry on his work. So the ball is in our court.

As Luke says, in the first reading for Ascension Sunday, "In the first book [i.e., the gospel], Theophilus, I wrote about all that Jesus did and taught from the beginning until the day when he was taken up to heaven, after giving instructions through the Holy Spirit to the apostles whom he had chosen." Jesus has done his part.

Luke goes on, in the same reading, to tell how Jesus announced the work that he intended his apostles and us to do: "You will receive power when the Holy Spirit has come upon you; and you will be my witnesses in Jerusalem, in all Judea and Samaria, and to the ends of the earth." We have our work cut out for us!

Thank goodness for the prayer Paul breathes for us in the second reading: "I pray that the God of our Lord Jesus Christ, the Father of glory, may give you a spirit of wisdom and revelation as you come to know him, so that, with the eyes of your heart enlightened, you may know what is the hope to which he has called you, what are the riches of his glorious inheritance among the saints, and what is the immeasurable greatness of his power for us who believe, according to the working of his great power." This beautiful and inspiring prayer gives us courage.

The gospel clinches the matter. The risen Jesus says these last words to his apostles and to us: "Go therefore and make disciples of all nations, baptizing them in the name of the Father and of the Son and of the Holy Spirit, and teaching them to obey everything that I have commanded you. And remember, I am with you always, to the end of the age."

The gospel of Matthew has no ascension account. He wants us to realize that though we must now take action, the risen Jesus remains with us always. With the help of the Holy Spirit we can fulfil the task Jesus gave us. No doubt about it.

1. Name a time when all preparations for a particular task were done and you, or your group, were left to carry it out.
2. How did Jesus prepare us for the task of making disciples for him the world over?
3. Reflect on Paul's prayer in the second reading.
4. What can you do as an individual to spread the gospel?

Pentecost

Acts 2:1-11
1 Corinthians 12:3b-7, 12-13
John 20:19-23

Challenges Beyond Our Own Capacity

If you had a voice only a mother could love, how would you like being challenged to take a leading role in an opera? If you couldn't run faster than a snail, how would you feel about being asked to join Canada's Olympic track team?

These examples are exaggerated, but there are times when we are asked to do something for which we feel entirely unqualified. The readings for last Sunday, Ascension, challenged us to take the good news to the whole world. Lest such a task seem beyond the power of his followers, Jesus told them to wait until the Spirit came. We celebrate the coming of the Spirit this Sunday, on the feast of Pentecost.

The first reading tells us how the Holy Spirit descended on Jesus' followers and how they reacted. They heard a powerful wind from heaven and then "divided tongues, as of fire, appeared among them, and a tongue rested on each of them." They all "began to speak in other languages, as the Spirit gave them ability."

Through the Spirit they now possessed the power and the ability to share the good news with all the nations of the world.

In the second reading Paul explains what the Spirit does for us. First, the Spirit enables us to say, "Jesus is Lord." Only with the Spirit's help can we come to realize and acknowledge that Jesus is indeed God. Of ourselves we cannot arrive at such a truth.

Paul then goes on to say, "Now there are varieties of gifts but the same Spirit; and there are varieties of services, but the same Lord…. To each is given the manifestation of the Spirit for the common good."

The Holy Spirit thus facilitates and coordinates all the activities of Christians so that they can accomplish God's purpose for the world.

In the gospel John adds another dimension to what the Spirit gives us. Upon appearing to his followers on "the first day of the week," Jesus says: "Receive the Holy Spirit. If you forgive the sins of any, they are forgiven them; if you retain the sins of any, they are retained."

Through the Spirit the Church possesses the power to forgive sin. As Christians we too are to forgive and heal one another. Too often we forget we have this power.

Though we are given the great challenge to bring all peoples to Christ, we cannot do this by ourselves. We can do it only in and through the Spirit. And the Spirit will always keep us focused on our mission.

1. Describe an experience of being challenged in a way that you felt was beyond your abilities. What happened?
2. Think about how the apostles, most of whom were uneducated, went out and, through the Spirit, fulfilled Jesus' command to share the good news. In light of their example, how can we do the same?
3. There are varieties of gifts in each Christian community. How can you, as an individual and as part of a group, exercise your gifts?
4. How can you, as an individual, exercise the power of forgiveness given to you through the Spirit?

Trinity Sunday

Exodus 34:4b-6, 8-9
2 Corinthians 13:11-13
John 3:16-18

The Higher the Better

I once heard someone remark that when you have a problem with a business concern, the higher up the executive ladder you go the better you are received. This often seems to be true. The fact is that employees at lower levels sometimes do not have the understanding and vision of those at higher levels.

Though this principle doesn't hold in all cases, we can be sure that going to the very top in matters of faith always produces results. The reason is simple. God is so good, so understanding, so compassionate. We, on the other hand, can often be petty, narrow-minded and hard-hearted.

That God is one to whom we can go in all confidence is borne out by the readings for this Sunday, the feast of the Trinity.

The first reading tells of Moses' second ascent to Mt. Sinai. He had met God there once before when he received the Ten Commandments, God's covenant with the people. When Moses brought this covenant to the people he found them worshipping a golden calf. That is why he ascended Mt. Sinai a second time – to plead with God for his guilty people.

What kind of reception does Moses get? A God raging at the sin of the people's flagrant idolatry? Far from it. God proclaims: "The Lord, the Lord, a God merciful and gracious, slow to anger, and abounding in steadfast love and faithfulness." Encouraged by these words, Moses pleads that the people be forgiven.

In the second reading Paul bids the Corinthians to "agree with one another, live in peace; and the God of love and peace will be with you." He concludes, "The grace of the Lord Jesus Christ, the love of God, and the communion of the Holy Spirit be with all of you."

Again, God comes to us as one who radiates love and peace.

In the gospel Jesus says to Nicodemus, "God so loved the world that he gave his only Son, so that everyone who believes in him may not perish but may have eternal life. Indeed God did not send his Son into the world to condemn the world, but in order that the world might be saved through him."

Clearly God is most approachable: tender, compassionate, kind, loving, forgiving, slow to anger and infinitely generous.

Pray then that you and I, as God's representatives and witnesses to the Son and Spirit, may show the same qualities to all who approach us.

1. Describe a few of your experiences of approaching God when you are having difficulties.
2. Reflect on God's response to Moses in the first reading.
3. In addition to bringing our troubles to God, how else are we to face them? (Paul gives us some hints in the second reading.)
4. How do you see God's loving compassion at its highest in giving us Jesus?

Body and Blood of Christ

Deuteronomy 8:2-3, 14b-16
1 Corinthians 10:16-17
John 6:51-59

Fast-Food Fads

With so many fast foods on the market today, and their link to increasing levels of obesity, diabetes and heart disease, people are becoming increasingly conscious of the need for a healthy diet. This is good. Our bodies deserve to be treated well.

Our minds and spirits do, too. We need to be on the lookout for mind and spirit nourishment, because now more than ever, many of this world's offerings are anything but life-giving. Ponder on the readings for this coming Sunday, the feast of Corpus Christi. They tell us about the wondrous food God provides, a food which alone can bring us to the fullness of our humanity.

The first reading, from the Old Testament, foreshadows the truly substantial food to be given in New Testament times. Amidst the trials and difficulties of their desert journey, the Hebrews are at their wits' end. Extremely hungry, they suddenly come upon a new source of nourishment, which they call "manna." God gave them this food, as the author of Deuteronomy says, "In order to make you understand that one does not live by bread alone, but by every word that comes from the mouth of the Lord."

In the second reading Paul speaks of the food that the manna prefigured. "The cup of blessing that we bless, is it not a sharing in the blood of Christ? The bread that we break, is it not a sharing in the body of Christ?"

At the Passover meal, Jewish people ate the Paschal lamb and drank the wine in memory of their deliverance from Egypt. Now, in New Testament times, we eat and drink of the new Paschal lamb, Jesus, who delivers us from sin.

In the gospel Jesus states, "I am the living bread that came down from heaven. Whoever eats of this bread will live forever.... Unless you eat the flesh of the Son of Man and drink his blood you have no life in you. Those who eat my flesh and drink my blood have eternal life, and I will raise them up on the last day."

These are extraordinary words! They promise that in and through the Eucharist we are being introduced into an ever-closer union with Christ and with one another. This is a promise the world cannot make. However, the Eucharist, like all interpersonal relationships, works mysteriously, not magically. To participate fully in this meal from heaven we must constantly strive to put on the mind and heart of Christ. The more we do so, the more nourishment we will receive from the Eucharist.

So amidst the fast-food fads and media glut of today, remember the one food and drink that enables us to grow into the fullness of being human.

～❀～

1. How do you strive to improve your mind and heart?
2. How is the Jewish Passover meal a forerunner of the Eucharist?
3. Why is the Eucharist such a fulfilling meal?
4. What word or phrase from the readings will you carry with you this week?

Tenth Sunday in Ordinary Time

Hosea 6:3-6
Romans 4:18-25
Matthew 9:9-13

Hearts Are Trump

In the great arena of human life hearts are trump. Scientific discoveries, technological advances, great art and music and literature are all wonderful achievements. They indeed increase our quality of life. But they will all come to nought unless the human heart is in tune. And the human heart can only be in tune through love.

Unless we deeply love one another, the human race will fall apart. As we are reminded in this Sunday's readings, the source of all love is God, for God is love.

In the first reading, the prophet Hosea calls the people of God to much-needed repentance. They have become far too mechanical in their relationship with God. Their liturgies are stilted and dry. So Hosea says in God's name, "I desire steadfast love and not sacrifice, the knowledge of God rather than burnt offerings."

In the second reading Paul makes clear to the Christians in Rome that just as Abraham believed in God's promise that Abraham would become "the father of many nations" despite his advanced age, so Christians are to have a deep, unwavering faith in God. Such faith is the foundation of love.

In the gospel Jesus paraphrases the words of Hosea from the first reading: "I desire mercy, not sacrifice." Mercy is a daughter of love. Only a loving heart can be truly merciful.

We come back, then, to love as the only solid basis for an ever better world. For where love is, there is God. God is love. Truly, then, hearts are trump in this game of life.

~⊗~

1. Describe an experience when love has played an important role in your life.
2. Reflect on the idea that mercy is a daughter of love. What other qualities spring from love?
3. What can move us to greater love?
4. What word or phrase from the readings will you carry with you this week?

Eleventh Sunday in Ordinary Time

Exodus 19:1-6a
Romans 5:6-11
Matthew 9:36–10:8

A Priestly Kingdom

In many countries of the world today, including Canada and the United States, there is a shortage of ordained priests. What are we to do?

Several solutions are being proposed. Not all will be accepted. And those that are accepted will take considerable time to implement. So the question remains – what can we do in the meantime?

The first reading for this coming Sunday, as well as the gospel, touches on an answer: "You shall be for me a priestly kingdom." Some translations are more explicit. The New American Bible puts it this way: "You shall be to me a kingdom of priests." The gospel emphasizes the need for labourers: "The harvest is plentiful, but the labourers are few."

In the *Catechism of the Catholic Church* we read, "The whole community of believers is, as such, priestly. The faithful exercise their baptismal priesthood through their participation...in Christ's mission as priest, prophet and king" (§ 1546).

All the baptized, then, are priests – not ordained priests, yet truly priests participating in the very mission of Christ.

So perhaps the present shortage of ordained priests is a blessing in disguise. A few years ago, who would have thought that today's faithful would be ministering in so many new ways?

This challenge to all the faithful is not just a stop-gap solution. It's part of our tradition. From now on, even if the shortage of ordained priests is lessened, all the faithful will be called upon to ever greater exercise of their priesthood. What a wonderful opportunity!

~❧~

1. Reflect on the idea of the "priesthood of all the faithful." What does this mean to you as a baptized Christian?
2. Every baptized person has gifts to offer. How could a parish make use of these gifts?
3. Try to name your own gifts and talents. How could they be used in the community?
4. What word or phrase from the readings will you carry with you this week?

Twelfth Sunday in Ordinary Time

Jeremiah 20:7, 10-13
Romans 5:12-15
Matthew 10:26-33

Knocking Knees

From last Sunday's readings we learned that all the faithful participate through their baptism in the mission of Christ. All are sent to act as priests, prophets and kings. That's what Jesus did in his public ministry. So that's what we must do.

Do I mean that even the laity must intercede for people, must speak for God and become kings through loving service? Yes! That is what you and I are to do, even though it sends our knees a-knocking.

However, help is at hand. It's as close as this Sunday's readings.

The first reading, from the prophet Jeremiah, reminds us that when we speak God's truth, look out! Someone is going to resent us. Jeremiah quickly found that out. People reacted to his teachings by saying, "Let us denounce him!" As Jeremiah says, even his close friends were watching for him to stumble.

The reason why God's truth meets objection is clear from the second reading. Paul says, "Sin came into the world through one man." This sin, with its consequent death, Paul says, "spread to all." Sin brings out perversity.

Now, we sinners don't like to be reminded of our sin. But reminded we must be, otherwise we remain in it. Sin finds remedy only through and in Christ.

The gospel encourages us in our commission to speak in God's name. Jesus says to us, "Have no fear.... What I say to you in the dark, tell in the light; and what you hear whispered, proclaim from the housetops."

The gospel adds a final boost to our courage. "Everyone therefore who acknowledges me before others, I also will acknowledge before my Father in heaven."

So despite our knocking knees, we must continue witnessing to Christ.

❦

1. Describe experiences you've had, whether good or not so good, of standing up for your faith.
2. Name different ways of witnessing to Christ that will attract and encourage people.
3. What ways of witnessing have you found to be effective?
4. What word or phrase from the readings will you carry with you this week?

Thirteenth Sunday in Ordinary Time

2 Kings 4:8-12a, 14-17
Romans 6:3-4, 8-11
Matthew 10:37-42

Give or Gimme?

One of the not-so-good effects of our present civilization is a "gimme" mentality. Today's marketplace is filled with a plethora of consumer goods. Newspapers, magazines, radio and TV display and promote them relentlessly, so of course we desire those products. Hence a "gimme" mentality.

How can we counteract such a selfish slant on life? We need look no further than the readings for this Sunday. They are not only a powerful antidote to selfishness but they make it crystal clear that it is indeed more blessed to give than to receive.

In the first reading a certain wealthy woman notices that the prophet Elisha frequently passed through her village. The woman suggests to her husband that they fix up accommodations for him in their home, and so they did. In thanksgiving Elisha gives them a precious promise: "At this season, in due time, you shall embrace a son."

In the gospel Jesus, as he so often did, turns worldly values upside down. "Those who find their life will lose it, and those who lose their life for my sake will find it." The reading concludes with Jesus' promise that "whoever gives even a cup of cold water to one of these little ones...none of these will lose their reward."

In the second reading Paul offers us a solid reason for giving in Jesus' name: that we are "baptized into his death." That is, just as Jesus gave his very life for us and was raised in resurrection, we, in giving of ourselves now, live by resurrection life (coming to fullness only in death).

Listening to and absorbing this Sunday's readings will enable us to free ourselves from this world's "gimme" spirit.

❧❀❧

1. Describe a time when you were caught up in the "gimme" net.
2. How do the readings for this Sunday help free us from the "gimme" spirit?
3. How can we implement the lesson of the readings in our lives?
4. What word or phrase from the readings will you carry with you this week?

Fourteenth Sunday in Ordinary Time

Zechariah 9:9-10
Romans 8:9, 11-13
Matthew 11:25-30

To Whom Should We Listen?

Today we are overwhelmed by the media. Voices by the thousands clamour for our attention: voices on television and radio, voices in print. We simply cannot hear and read them all. We must make choices.

The problem is, how do we determine what is worthwhile and what is not? This Sunday's readings come to our aid, offering excellent criteria on how to make good judgments in this matter.

In the first reading, the prophet Zechariah speaks of one to come who will be victorious, yet humble: so humble, indeed, that he will come not on a warrior's steed but "riding on a donkey." And he will proclaim peace.

We know that Zechariah's words were fulfilled in Jesus. Though lowly and humble, Jesus gained the greatest of victories: victory over evil.

In the second reading Paul tells the Romans, "You are not in the flesh; you are in the Spirit, since the Spirit of God dwells in you." He continues, "But if by the Spirit you put to death the deeds of the body, you will live." It is the Spirit who gives us life.

The gospel is even more to the point. Jesus thanks his Father for hiding his wisdom from the wise and the intelligent and revealing it to infants. This is a clear indication that only the humble are good listeners. Those who are learned and proud are a voice unto themselves.

Jesus continues, "No one knows the Father except the Son and anyone to whom the Son chooses to reveal him." It is only in God that our hearts will find rest. That is why Jesus concludes with these words: "Come to me, all you that are weary...and I will give you rest."

Thus the words of Jesus, as taught by the Church, are the ultimate criteria of truth as well as being the basic direction in life. All other words we hear or read must be in accord with the thought of Jesus.

⌒⊛⌒

1. What are the voices directed at you today, demanding your attention? How do you decide which ones deserve to be heard?
2. Why does true wisdom come only from the mouth of a humble person?
3. Reflect on Paul's words: "You are not in the flesh; you are in the Spirit, since the Spirit of God dwells in you."
4. Reflect on these words of Jesus: "Learn from me; for I am gentle and humble in heart...my yoke is easy, and my burden is light." What does this mean in your life?

Fifteenth Sunday in Ordinary Time

Isaiah 55:10-11
Romans 8:18-23
Matthew 13:1-23

An Investor's Dream

In the world of commerce, those with money look for good investments. If a particular venture has promise of quick riches, well and good. But financial types are usually wary. Most prefer solid investments rather than the pie-in-the-sky variety. Even if an investment's reward is a long-term affair, that's all right.

God is also an investor. As the first reading from Isaiah indicates, God sends down the rain and snow to water the earth and expects the earth to yield an abundance. But more importantly, God expects the word that comes out of his mouth to "accomplish that which I purpose."

In the second reading Paul informs the Christians of Rome that God has long-term plans for humans and for their world. Even though physical creation "was subjected to futility," nevertheless it "will be set free from its bondage to decay and will obtain the freedom of the glory of the children of God."

The gospel is the familiar parable of the sower and the seed. The sower plants in various types of soil. The seeds falling on poor soil fail to mature. But those on good soil yield a huge return – some a hundredfold, others sixtyfold and others thirtyfold. What an abundant increase!

(How often have you heard of a 100 per cent, or even a 30 per cent, return on an investment?)

These readings show that God truly expects a great payoff from his investment in humanity and in the universe. To ensure such a payoff, God takes "hands-on" care of us and our world. He cares for us with love, patience and forgiveness.

Our part is to co-operate wholeheartedly with God, for we know that God's investments will not fail.

∽❀∼

1. Describe experiences you've had in investing – in the stock market, in a business venture or, better yet, in people.
2. How is God a master investor?
3. Reflect on the various ways we co-operate with God in enriching earthly life and in enriching people.
4. What word or phrase from the readings will you carry with you this week?

Sixteenth Sunday in Ordinary Time

Wisdom 12:13, 16-19
Romans 8:26-27
Matthew 13:24-43

Good Management

Today more than ever, the world is discovering that those in authority are most successful when they treat people who work for them with respect and with a clear recognition of their gifts and abilities.

Long before the world learned the way of good management, God, our creator, and God's Son, our redeemer, exemplified it. What's more, God gives us the necessary strength to follow his lead. Only in heeding God's example and accepting the strength we need can we avoid the dangers of authoritarianism and become the best of managers.

In the first reading, from the Book of Wisdom, the author begins by acknowledging that there is no one comparable to God, "whose care is for all people." The author then says this about God: "Although you are sovereign in strength, you judge with mildness, and with great forbearance you govern us."

In the second reading Paul also acknowledges how God helps us out: "The Spirit helps us in our weakness."

The gospel is the parable of weeds among the wheat. The sower "sowed good seed in his field."

But an enemy "sowed weeds among the wheat." Jesus compares the kingdom of heaven to one who sows wheat in his field. An enemy comes along and sows weeds in the same field. When the wheat and weeds both sprout, the farm help brings this to the owner's attention. How does the owner react? Instead of venting his anger at the enemy, he advises his workers to let the weeds grow, for fear that in uprooting them they might damage the wheat. At harvest time the wheat and weeds will be separated: the former put into sheds and the latter burned.

God is thus one who fully recognizes our weakness but deals with us wisely, gently and with forbearance.

～֎～

1. Describe an incident where those in authority used their position unwisely or wisely.
2. Sometimes we think of God as a forbidding God, a God who judges us harshly. How do this Sunday's readings prove this to be wrong?
3. Why do you think God is kind to us in our weakness?
4. What word or phrase from the readings will you carry with you this week?

Seventeenth Sunday in Ordinary Time

1 Kings 3:5-12
Romans 8:28-30
Matthew 13:44-52

The Cheerful Giver

We've all met people who willingly share their talents and possessions with others, asking for nothing in return. Indeed, we've coined a phrase to describe a generous person: "They'd give you the shirt off their back." We like such cheerful givers.

On the other hand, we've all met the more stingy types, those who seldom give of themselves or of their possessions. We instinctively know that such an attitude is wrong.

This Sunday's readings, which show us that God is the most selfless of givers, teach us to be likewise.

In the first reading God, upon being asked, is happy to give King Solomon a share of divine wisdom.

In the second reading, Paul assures the Romans that God looks after those who love God. Indeed, God wants us "to be conformed to the image of his Son." In other words, God wants to share his inner life with us. He wants us to be part of the divine family. What more could God do for us or share with us?

In the gospel Jesus gives wonderful examples of God's generosity. He compares God's kingdom, to which we are all invited, to a treasure hidden in a field. Someone finds this treasure and sells all his possessions in order to buy that property (and so acquire the treasure).

God's kingdom is also like a merchant who comes across one pearl of great value. He sells all he has in order to buy the pearl.

Jesus gives a third example: God's kingdom is like a net cast into the sea, catching fish of every kind. Like the wheat and the weeds of last Sunday's gospel, some fish are good, others not. Only at end-time will they finally be separated. In the meantime, there is opportunity for repentance.

God, who loves a cheerful giver, is the richest and most cheerful of all givers.

❧

1. Describe a time when you or someone you know received something from a cheerful giver.
2. In the second reading, Paul clearly outlines God's generosity to us. What do his words mean to you?
3. God's kingdom, exemplified in this Sunday's gospel, is pure gift to us. What is your reaction to this gift?
4. What word or phrase from the readings will you carry with you this week?

Eighteenth Sunday in Ordinary Time

Isaiah 55:1-3
Romans 8:35, 37-39
Matthew 14:13-21

The Banquet of Banquets

We humans are body/spirit people. When we express our thoughts, we use physical symbols – words, actions, sounds, colours, and so on.

Amongst all the symbols we use, one of the richest and most meaningful is that of a banquet. Food and drink are the necessities of life. In celebrating important occasions we naturally offer a sumptuous meal, a banquet.

It's no wonder that the inspired writers of sacred scripture use the image of a banquet to express God's bountiful relationship with us. Each of the readings for this Sunday bears this out.

In the first reading Isaiah says, "Listen carefully to me, and eat what is good, and delight yourselves in rich food. Incline your ear, and come to me; listen, so that you may live."

In the second reading Paul exclaims to the Christians of Rome: "Who will separate us from the love of Christ? Will hardship, or distress, or persecution, or famine, or nakedness, or peril, or sword?" Nothing, he continues, "will be able to separate us from the love of God in Christ Jesus our Lord."

While Paul doesn't use the banquet symbol here, he does stress what is at the very heart of what God gives us — a share in eternal love through Christ Jesus. Paul sees all of life, its joys and even its hardships, as a great banquet.

In the gospel Jesus feeds a hungry crowd of over five thousand with only five loaves and a few fish. "All ate and were filled." And twelve baskets were left over! Through this symbolic action Jesus makes it clear that in him all our needs will be abundantly satisfied.

The food Jesus gives is himself. And he gives of himself ever so generously to all who seek the truth.

⤙❀⤚

1. Recall and describe some of the happy times you've had at banquets.
2. The people of Israel imagined eternal life as a great banquet. Reflect on this image.
3. Share your understanding of how Jesus continues to "banquet" with us!
4. What word or phrase from the readings will you carry with you this week?

Nineteenth Sunday in Ordinary Time

1 Kings 19:9a, 11-13a
Romans 9: 1-5
Matthew 14:22-33

God Grows on Us Gradually

We humans come to know one another gradually: one experience at a time, and over a long period. Indeed, only after several such experiences, which continue over time, do we feel at home with one another.

In a similar way, God makes himself known to us gradually. In Old Testament times he revealed himself in various words and happenings throughout the long history of Israel. About 2000 years ago, God revealed himself through his only begotten Son, Jesus of Nazareth. This was as full a revelation as God in his wisdom saw fit to give us. In turn, the Son committed himself to the Church to live out his words and work until the end of time.

In the first reading Elijah finds God in an unexpected place: in the sound of a gentle breeze, not in earthquakes and fire.

In the second reading Paul, who was temporarily blinded by his encounter with the Risen Christ on the road to Damascus, anguishes over Israel's blindness to the miracles and teachings of Jesus.

In the gospel, the disciples are caught in a violent storm while crossing the sea of Galilee.

Jesus comes walking to them on the storm-tossed water. They think he is a ghost and cry out in fear. Jesus challenges Peter to walk towards him. Peter starts out but becomes frightened and begins to sink. He cries out, "Lord, save me!" Jesus reaches out to him and says, "You of little faith, why did you doubt?"

Like Peter we, too, have our frightening moments. We doubt. This is part of our growth; through doubting we get to know Jesus better when, like Peter, we confess Jesus as Lord and come to a deeper faith.

～❀～

1. Describe an experience of coming to know someone gradually.
2. How does this help us to get to know one another?
3. How has God gradually revealed himself to you?
4. What word or phrase from the readings will you carry with you this week?

Twentieth Sunday in Ordinary Time

Isaiah 56:1, 6-7
Romans 11:13-15, 29-32
Matthew 15:21-28

Insiders/Outsiders

One of the darker sides of our humanity is our tendency to be exclusive. We build our own little world and God help those who disturb it! We also tend to join exclusive groups. New members are only grudgingly accommodated.

Thanks to God for being the exact opposite! God is totally and forever inclusive. All humans are God's beloved children. If some are not, it's their decision, not God's.

This inclusiveness of God is well exemplified in this Sunday's readings.

In the first reading, Isaiah, speaking for God, says this: All who join themselves to the Lord "will be brought to my holy mountain." There are no exceptions.

In the second reading, Paul voices his pleasure in being sent to the Gentiles. He concludes with this powerful statement: "For God has imprisoned all in disobedience so that he may be merciful to all." (God did not cause the imprisonment. We did. But God effects a merciful freedom.)

In the gospel Jesus speaks openly with a pagan woman, who asks him to cure her daughter. At first Jesus seems to refuse, saying, "I was sent only to the lost sheep of the house of Israel." But the woman persists, noting that even dogs feed on the crumbs from their master's table. Jesus, recognizing her faith and humility, says, "Let it be done for you as you wish."

To God there are no outsiders. He loves us all, and he pursues us relentlessly. The poet Francis Thompson called God "The Hound of Heaven." He pursues all of us and never gives up.

~❀~

1. What is behind an "in-group" mentality?
2. Reflect on Jesus' relationship with the Pharisees of his day.
3. Give a few examples of Jesus' openness to all peoples.
4. What word or phrase from the readings will you carry with you this week?

Twenty-first Sunday in Ordinary Time

Isaiah 22:15, 19-23
Romans 11:33-36
Matthew 16:13-20

Divine Promotions

In the course of ordinary life, everyone has been promoted at one time. We have all been promoted from one grade to the next, and many of us have received promotions in our place of work or in other organizations to which we belonged.

In most cases, I dare say, we have earned it. And we feel good about it. This experience helps us better appreciate the readings for this Sunday.

In the first reading Isaiah has been asked to relay God's message to Shebna. Shebna is to relinquish his office of prime minister of the kingdom, and Eliakim is to take over. We can read between the lines and conclude that Shebna has not been doing a good job. Eliakim, however, "shall be a father to the inhabitants of Jerusalem."

In the gospel, Peter the apostle receives the highest position among the followers of Jesus. Jesus pronounces Peter as the rock on which "I will build my church." Moreover, Jesus says, "I will give you the keys of the kingdom of heaven." And, like Eliakim in the first reading, Peter has the power of binding and loosening.

Lest we wonder whether God chooses the right person on which to confer power, the second reading assures us, through Paul, of "the riches and wisdom and knowledge of God!"

～❁～

1. Describe some of your experiences of being promoted. How did you feel?
2. Put yourself in Eliakim's shoes. How could you be an honour "to his ancestral house"?
3. Reflect on Paul's wonderful praise of God in the second reading.
4. What word or phrase from the readings will you carry with you this week?

Twenty-second Sunday
in Ordinary Time

Jeremiah 20:7-9
Romans 12:1-2
Matthew 16:21-27

Giftedness Calls for Giving

We are all given gifts by God, and are called to use these gifts in our daily lives. Take the medical profession as an example. Doctors have the gift of healing. To exercise this gift properly, they must first undergo long years of training. Once they have their M.D., they devote themselves to healing the sick. This means long and difficult hours in their office and in hospital. True, they receive good pay. Their greatest reward, however, is to see their patients' health improve.

This example helps us appreciate the readings for this Sunday. The truth is that all of us are gifted by God both in our natural and spiritual lives. And all of us are called to be of service to others.

In the first reading the prophet Jeremiah reminds us that being a prophet was no cakewalk. It was hard! Yet when he is tempted to stop prophesying, he says, "a burning fire shut up in my bones." Jeremiah's prophecies still inspire us to this day.

In the second reading Paul tells the Christians in Rome to "present your bodies as a living sacrifice." God's gift of self to us prompts us to return that gift by sacrificing ourselves for God and for others. This is our "living sacrifice," our giving of self.

In the gospel Jesus teaches that great failure awaits us if we do not use our giftedness for the good of others, saying, "For those who want to save their life will lose it, and those who lose their life for my sake will find it."

There is no doubt that our giftedness is for Christ and so for others.

⮌⟜❀⟊⮎

1. Describe a time when your service to others gave you real happiness.
2. Reflect on Jeremiah's words in the first reading. Keep in mind that he continued to prophesy up to his death.
3. How do we present our bodies as "a living sacrifice," as Paul teaches in the second reading?
4. Think about Jesus' words in the gospel about losing and gaining our life. What does he mean?

Twenty-third Sunday in Ordinary Time

Ezekiel 33:7-9
Romans 13:8-10
Matthew 18:15-20

Guards Galore

Many groups in the animal kingdom set up guards while they are feeding. Canada geese do, as do mountain goats.

We humans also have guards. Parents act as guards for their children. The military uses guards extensively. Many businesses have both day and night security guards.

What about the Christian community? Do we have guards? Assuredly we do. Our faith is far too precious a reality to be left open for anyone to despoil. This very concern is addressed in the readings for this Sunday.

Ezekiel spent his earlier years pointing out to his people the infidelities that had led to their exile in Babylon. Now he takes on a new role. The exile is almost over. God appoints him to be a guardian for Israel. God says to him, "So you, O mortal, I have made a sentinel for the house of Israel...you shall give them warning from me." Were he not to take this appointment seriously, Ezekiel knows he would be responsible for harm coming to those whom he failed to warn.

In the second reading Paul says that the commandments "are summed up in this word, 'Love your neighbour as yourself.'" Love for God and neighbour is the foundation for all Christian action. Because we love our neighbours we look out for them. We guard them. If they go astray, we warn them. If our love was not evident to them, such warnings would be empty and ineffectual.

In the gospel Jesus tells us explicitly how we are to care for others. "If your brother or sister sins against you, go and point out the fault when the two of you are alone. If the brother or sister listens to you, you have regained that one. But if you are not listened to, take one or two others along with you, so that every word may be confirmed." In other words, every effort must be made to free those who are caught up in wrongdoing.

We Christians are thus called upon to be "guards," for our Christian family and for the whole human community. We cannot leave this responsibility only to the hierarchy and to theologians. True, the latter two groups have a special role in standing watch. But all Christians share in this responsibility, each according to her or his particular gifts, abilities and circumstances.

As "guards," the good we do will always be in proportion to the depth of our love.

1. What are your everyday experiences of being a "lookout" for others?
2. How is love the solid basis for being a "lookout?"
3. What difficulties do we meet when we warn others of the dangers they face if they continue on a wrong path?
4. It is difficult to be a good lookout. How can you fulfill this role responsibly?

Twenty-fourth Sunday
in Ordinary Time

Sirach 27:30–28:7
Romans 14:7-9
Matthew 18:21-35

Stepping on Toes

Wherever people gather, some toes are going to be stepped on. It's simply part of the give and take of life, for we are not angels but humans. That means we aren't perfect – yet.

You can take it for granted that somewhere, somehow, and by someone, you are going to be trampled upon. The danger is that when this happens, you'll become angry and resentful. The better part of valour, then, is to nip anger and resentment in the bud. How? This Sunday's readings give us the answer.

In the first reading Sirach says, "Anger and wrath, these are abominations.... The vengeful will face the Lord's vengeance.... Forgive your neighbour the wrong that is done.... Does anyone harbour anger against another, and expect healing from the Lord?"

In the second reading Paul states, "We do not live to ourselves, and we do not die to ourselves." What each of us does affects others. That's how Jesus redeems us! Jesus also affords us a model for dealing with one another.

In the gospel Jesus, answering Peter's question about how often we are to forgive others, tells a parable about the king who wished to settle accounts with his slaves. One owed him such a vast amount of money that he had no way of paying up. Out of pity for him, "the lord of that slave released him and forgave him the debt."

The same servant, upon meeting one of his fellows who owed him a small amount of money, will not listen to his pleas for mercy. Indeed, he immediately puts the fellow into prison until the debt is taken care of. Upon hearing this, the master is furious. Forthwith he "handed him over to be tortured until he would pay his entire debt." Jesus then draws the moral: "So my heavenly Father will also do to every one of you, if you do not forgive your brother or sister from your heart."

A powerful parable indeed!

To avoid further anger and resentment arising from being stepped on, the old maxim about an ounce of prevention comes in handy. And the "ounce" in this case is a constant attitude of forgiveness. With such an attitude, anger and resentments won't pile up but will be washed away in mercy's flood.

1. To feel angry and resentful is not wrong; but to nurture such feelings is wrong. Describe a few of your experiences of being trespassed against or even of trespassing against others.
2. Name several ways of controlling anger and resentment that you have found helpful.
3. Reflect on God's mercy towards us.
4. What word or phrase from the readings will you carry with you this week?

Twenty-fifth Sunday in Ordinary Time

Isaiah 55:6-9
Philippians 1:20c-24, 27
Matthew 20:1-16

"It Can't Be Done"

We no sooner say, "It can't be done," than someone goes ahead and does it. Or we say, "It shouldn't be done that way, it won't work," and someone does it exactly that way and it does work. We are embarrassed, of course, and well we should be, for our own talents and ways are not the measure of human capacity. Others have different abilities and different ways. More importantly, God's powers and God's ways are vastly different from our own, as this Sunday's readings show.

In the first reading, Isaiah addresses a group of dispirited Jewish exiles. They think that Israel's dream has come to an end. Even though King Cyrus of Persia, now the conqueror of Babylon, had allowed them to return to their native land, still, what could they possibly do with the rubble pile that was Jerusalem?

God, as Isaiah makes clear, was not deterred by his people's pessimism. God reminds them that his ways and thoughts are different from theirs. And God can pull things off where they cannot. "For my thoughts are not your thoughts, nor are your ways my ways.... For as the heavens are higher than the earth, so are my ways higher than your ways, and my thoughts than your thoughts."

In the second reading Paul makes a similar point. In deliberating about his future he thinks that if it were left up to him alone, he would prefer an early death so as to be fully with Christ. But, he realizes, that may not be what God wants of him. And what God wants is most important for Paul. So he is entirely reconciled to the thought of staying on earth in order to give further help to his converts.

The gospel is the familiar parable of a landowner who hires people at different hours of the day and yet at day's end pays them all the same wage.

This parable came as a shock to Jesus' listeners, as indeed it is for us. It was assumed that landowners should pay less to those who worked less. That makes good economic sense. But Jesus had a lesson to teach. He has the landowner say to the dissenters, "Am I not allowed to do what I choose with what belongs to me? Or are you envious because I am generous? So the last will be first, and the first will be last."

The landowner is God. We are the workers. We cannot put limits on God. We mustn't think that God thinks and acts like we do; God doesn't. Rather, like Paul, we are to seek out what God wants of us. If what God wants seems impossible, if it seems foolish, if it goes against our wishes, no matter. We should try to do it. And God being with us, it will be done.

⌒❀⌒

1. Give a few examples where someone said a task was impossible, but others went ahead and did it.
2. What does the parable of the landowner mean when applied to your life?
3. How do we go about discovering God's will for us?
4. What word or phrase from the readings will you carry with you this week?

Twenty-sixth Sunday in Ordinary Time

Ezekiel 18:25-28
Philippians 2:1-11
Matthew 21:28-32

The Smallness Within

There is a kind of "smallness" within each of us. We are jealous when others get ahead of us. We are stingy in our praise of others. We blame others when things don't go our way. At times we blame God.

We need an occasional jolt to help us break out of our petty horizons, our narrowness of heart. This Sunday's readings offer just such a jolt.

The first reading speaks about the Jewish exiles in Babylon who would not accept blame for their tragic plight. They accuse God of acting unjustly by allowing them to be taken into exile. Through the prophet Ezekiel God throws this accusation right back in their faces. "Hear now, O house of Israel: Is my way unfair? Is it not your ways that are unfair?" God then points out that when upright persons turn to sin, they bring death upon themselves. On the other hand, when sinners renounce their sins, God opens his arms to them. The point is that we are responsible agents. Our choices influence our future.

In the second reading, Paul addresses the Philippians on the matter of getting along with each other. He says that the one thing they could do to make his joy complete is to be "of the same mind." He continues, "Do nothing from selfish ambition or conceit, but in humility regard others as better than yourselves." This was Paul's advice on how to get rid of any "smallness" and acquire an "open-arms" attitude.

In the gospel Jesus clashes with the religious authorities. They were smug, self-sufficient, closed-hearted and small. The only thing big about them was their mouths. To shake them out of such complacency Jesus says, "Truly I tell you, the tax collectors and the prostitutes are going into the kingdom of God ahead of you."

Now that was a real jolt! And it wasn't meant only for Jewish authorities. It's meant for us too. It is meant to hit us squarely in the solar plexus!

Jesus knew that prostitutes and other notorious sinners ordinarily do not cover up their guilt. They acknowledge it, and so are more likely to seek forgiveness. On the other hand, the smallness within us clings to a self-righteous mentality and so keeps us from full repentance.

Thank goodness that God's arms are wide open, even to those of us who are afflicted with smallness. God enfolds us in an embrace that squeezes the smallness out of us.

1. Describe some of the "smallnesses" you find within yourself.
2. The Jewish people in exile blamed God for their plight. Do you ever do the same? Give an example.
3. Paul's advice to the Philippians is excellent. How can you apply it to yourself?
4. What word or phrase from the readings will you carry with you this week?

Twenty-seventh Sunday
in Ordinary Time

Isaiah 5:1-7
Philippians 4:6-9
Matthew 21:33-43

Unrequited Love

Have you ever poured out your heart to someone, been well received, and later been utterly rejected? How saddening and difficult this is. It feels like the bottom has fallen out of life, and all sorts of turmoil sets in. An experience like this can help us appreciate this Sunday's readings.

The first reading, from the prophet Isaiah, is called "The Song of the Unfruitful Vineyard." God planted a vineyard, Israel. He tended it well, "dug it and cleared it of stones, and planted it with choice vines." At vintage time, "he expected it to yield grapes, but it yielded wild grapes."

Israel did not yield the fruit God had the right to expect. Instead, Israel spurned him. So God says through Isaiah, "And now I will tell you what I will do to my vineyard. I will remove its hedge...break down its wall.... I will make it a waste; it shall not be pruned or hoed.... I will also command the clouds that they rain no rain upon it."

Drastic treatment, you say. True, but it is treatment, not reprisal. God is not vindictive. He is abandoning Israel, but only for a time, and only that Israel might come to know how much it needs God. It's a hard way to learn, but sometimes it's the only way.

With this first reading as background, the gospel tells the parable of the vineyard. Again, the landowner plants his vines and diligently cares for them. Then "he leased it to tenants and went to another country." At vintage time he sends his servants to collect his rightful share of the fruits, but the tenants "seized his slaves and beat one, killed another, and stoned another." He sends other servants. These are dealt with the same way as the first ones. Finally, he sends his son. At this the tenants say, "This is the heir; come, let us kill him and get his inheritance."

Those hearing the parable were asked what the landowner should do. They answer, "He will put those wretches to a miserable death, and lease the vineyard to other tenants." Little did they realize they were sentencing themselves!

This was Matthew's way of telling the Jewish leaders of his day, together with their followers, that because they had not accepted Jesus, and because they had excluded Jewish Christians from their midst, God was turning his vineyard over to new tenants.

Christians are, of course, the new tenants. But before we congratulate ourselves we must ask whether as Church or as individuals we have lived up to our responsibilities. History and our own conscience forbid us to answer with an unqualified "Yes." That is why we need

Paul's advice from the second reading: "Finally, beloved, whatever is true, whatever is honourable, whatever is just, whatever is pure, whatever is pleasing, whatever is commendable, if there is any excellence and if there is anything worthy of praise, think about these things."

1. Have you or has someone you know ever experienced unrequited love, or put your heart into something and received nothing in return? What happened?
2. Name some of the things God did for the Israelites to help them grow as a people. (What God did for the Israelites he did for us, for they are our faith ancestors.)
3. Reflect on Paul's advice to his Christian converts in Philippi. What does it mean for you?
4. What word or phrase from the readings will you carry with you this week?

Twenty-eighth Sunday
in Ordinary Time

Isaiah 25:6-10a
Philippians 4:10-14, 19-20
Matthew 22:1-14

Unlimited Hope

In every human heart lies hope for ultimate happiness. This is true no matter which faith tradition we embrace, for hope springs from the depth of our humanity.

Depending on culture and belief, the ultimate realization of a deeply rooted hope goes by various names. Some call it Nirvana, others Valhalla. Still others look forward to perfect fulfillment, to ultimate success, to final victory. Christians tend to name our hope as eternal life, eternal rest, a great banquet, or simply heaven. All people possess some type of basic hope.

Christians are especially blessed, for we have clear assurance whence our hope comes, whither it is leading, and the solid foundation upon which it rests, as we are reminded in the readings for this Sunday.

In the first reading, Isaiah speaks of our final fulfillment in terms of a great banquet. "On this mountain the Lord of hosts will make for all peoples a feast of rich food, a feast of well-aged wines.... And he will destroy on this mountain the shroud that is cast over all peoples.... [H]e will swallow up death forever."

In the second reading, Paul confides to the Philippians how strongly he feels about the future. "I can do all things through him who strengthens me." He adds, in view of the way the Philippians had received him, "My God will fully satisfy every need of yours according to his riches in glory in Christ Jesus." Paul makes clear that Christian hope is founded in God through the risen Jesus. It can never fail.

In the gospel, Jesus tells us that "the kingdom of heaven may be compared to a king who gave a wedding banquet for his son." A larger number of those invited are not interested. They all have various excuses. Incensed, the master says to his servants, "Go therefore into the main streets, and invite everyone you find to the wedding banquet." The wedding hall is filled. (Some few come under false pretenses and are excluded.)

All three readings thus make the same point: ultimate victory is assured. God, who implants hope in the human heart, will see to its fulfillment, and see to it in a way that will exceed anything we could imagine.

This assurance is meant to help us now in this life. The gospels consistently make the point that eternal life (heaven) is already active within us. The seed is planted. We are to nourish it, treasure it, prize it highly. On the final day we will say, as the first reading indicates, "This is the Lord for whom we have waited; let us be glad and rejoice in his salvation."

⌒⊱❀⊰⌒

1. The three virtues of our Christian lives are faith, hope and love. What does hope mean to you?
2. What's the difference between hope and enthusiasm?
3. Though our ultimate hope is heaven, how does hope play an important part in our day-to-day lives?
4. Why is Christ the true summit of our hope?

Twenty-ninth Sunday in Ordinary Time

Isaiah 45:1, 4-6
1 Thessalonians 1:1-5b
Matthew 22:15-21

A Worrisome World

There is cause to worry about our world today. It seems set on a disaster course.

Powder kegs exist in all parts of our world. Light a match and there'll be a war. Look around, see the threat of HIV/AIDS, the severe economic crises, the growing crime rate, the suicides, drug and alcohol addictions, violence. You name it, the world has it.

Amidst these threats, it's refreshing to remember that God remains in control. God can turn bad news into good, as we see in this Sunday's readings.

The first reading, from Isaiah, was written at a time when the traumatic exile of the Jewish people in Babylon was nearing an end. The dark clouds were beginning to roll away and the sun of freedom to shine. Cyrus the Persian had just conquered Babylon and his policy was to let his subjects return to their own land.

With this happy policy in mind, Isaiah calls Cyrus the Lord's anointed (the only pagan ever to be given that title in all of scripture), because he recognized that God was using Cyrus for the good of Israel.

Speaking to Cyrus in God's name, Isaiah says, "I am the Lord, and there is no other.... I arm you...so that all may know...there is no one besides me."

The gospel is a familiar one. The Pharisees and the Herodians ask Jesus, "Is it lawful to pay taxes to the emperor, or not?" Jesus avoids the trap and then counsels them, "Give therefore to the emperor the things that are the emperor's, and to God the things that are God's."

The caesars of this world (that is, the authorities) have an important role to play in human affairs. But they are not to usurp the authority of God. When they do so, they come into conflict with God. And in the long run God will win out.

To keep our sanity in a world of such worrisome trends, we must keep in mind that God is in control, despite all appearances to the contrary. A worrisome trend is not the end of the matter. It is only part of the picture.

Christians today need to think and act in this worry-filled world in a way that earns the praise Paul gives to the Thessalonians in the second reading: "We always give thanks to God for all of you...constantly remembering...your work of faith and labour of love and steadfastness of hope in our Lord Jesus Christ."

1. Name some other growing threats in our world today.
2. Why doesn't God seem to take a more active role in all these threats to peace and well-being?
3. How and why are we to put our hope in Christ?
4. What word or phrase from the readings will you carry with you this week?

Thirtieth Sunday in Ordinary Time

Exodus 22:21-27
1 Thessalonians 1:5c-10
Matthew 22:34-40

Needed: New Life for Old Words

Words tend to wear out. They have only as much meaning as people give them. They don't stand on their own. As people change, so do words.

We face an especially grave danger today. We are living in a very secular age, an age that is whittling away at our faith-words and bringing them down to its own size. They no longer express the richness they once did.

Among the many casualties of this secularization process is the word "love." Our Christian faith gave love a new and astounding depth. Now that depth, that richness, is being eroded in our secular world. We need to hasten back to God's word. Only there will we rediscover the deep meaning of love. This Sunday's readings are a good place to start.

Although the first reading doesn't mention the word "love," it powerfully portrays love's true nature. "You shall not wrong or oppress a resident alien.... You shall not abuse any widow or orphan.... If you lend money to my people...you shall not exact interest from them." In other words, the book of Exodus tells us to treat the downtrodden and neglected with kindness and compassion. This is what love is all about.

The second reading also leaves out the word "love." But in it Paul praises the Thessalonians for their loving response to himself and to the Lord. "And you became imitators of us and of the Lord, for in spite of persecution you received the word with joy inspired by the Holy Spirit, so that you became an example to all believers."

To imitate Christ is primarily to love God and our neighbour with all our hearts.

The gospel does use the word "love," and uses it powerfully. On being asked which was the greatest commandment, Jesus answers, "'You shall love the Lord your God with all your heart, and with all your soul, and with all your mind.' This is the greatest and first commandment. And a second is like it: 'You shall love your neighbour as yourself.'"

With the above words Jesus sums up all the commandments. Love is thus the central part of our Christian lives. It is a burning torch for us to carry, a fire to cleanse, purify and strengthen us.

It is such love, and such love alone, that can restore the true meaning of the word "love" in our world. It is, and was meant to be, Christ's presence to humanity.

1. What is true love all about?
2. Think about how you have been loved. What have these experiences meant to you?
3. Why can we not love God without loving our neighbour?
4. What word or phrase from the readings will you carry with you this week?

Thirty-first Sunday in Ordinary Time

Malachi 1:14b–2:2b, 8-10
1 Thessalonians 2:7b-9, 13
Matthew 23:1-12

Be Careful of "Isms"

"Ism" is joined to the ending of many nouns in order to emphasize a constant and definite state of affairs. Depending on the noun to which it is attached, it can have a good meaning or a bad one.

Take the word "authoritarian." In ordinary usage this word refers to an abuse of authority. The "ism" attached underlines the abuse. This takes us to the very heart of this Sunday's readings, for each of the three deals with authority and its abuse.

Everyone exercises some form of authority. All leaders in government, business and religion are authorities. But so are parents, and all gifted people (and we are all gifted in some way). The readings for this Sunday therefore apply to all of us.

In the first reading, the prophet Malachi addresses the priests of his day with these severe words: "And now, O priests, this command is for you.... I will send the curse on you.... You have turned aside from the way; you have caused many to stumble by your instruction."

In the gospel Jesus said to the crowds, "The scribes and the Pharisees sit in Moses' chair;

therefore, do whatever they teach you and follow it; but do not do as they do, for they do not practice what they teach."

Harsh warnings for the priests of Old Testament times as well as for the scribes and Pharisees of Jesus' day!

Paul, however, in the second reading, gives us the positive side of exercising authority: "We were gentle among you, like a nurse tenderly caring for her own children."

Finally, at the end of the gospel, Jesus gives us the most important clue for the exercise of authority: "The greatest among you will be your servant." Jesus, the truly greatest, became our servant.

∽❀∼

1. Describe some experiences, both good and bad, of those who have wielded some authority in your life.
2. When should authority be exercised more firmly?
3. What lessons in exercising authority have you gained from this Sunday's readings?
4. What word or phrase from the readings will you carry with you this week?

Thirty-second Sunday in Ordinary Time

Wisdom 6:12-16
1 Thessalonians 4:13-18
Matthew 25:1-13

Seekers, Finders

From day one of creation, we humans have been "seekers." Our insatiable curiosity reaches to all corners of the physical universe. In modern times, this seeking has become more extensive than ever before. Scientists are set on discovering all the secrets of the atom and of the universe itself.

This is well and good. Science has much to offer for the betterment of life. But it is not the only search, nor is it the most important one. Far superior to it is the search for wisdom. Science is about physical reality, whereas wisdom is about a higher and deeper reality. This latter search forms the content of this Sunday's readings.

The first reading has this to say about wisdom: "Wisdom is radiant and unfading, and she is easily discerned by those who love her, and is found by those who seek her."

What is this wisdom that the sacred author extols so highly?

Paul teaches that all true wisdom is found in Christ. To know him, to love him, to follow him is the way of wisdom. That is why, in the second reading, Paul tells those Thessalonians who were worried about their dead, "For since we believe that Jesus died and rose again, even so, through Jesus, God will bring with him those who have died." Paul then goes on to explain how Jesus will return at end-time.

True wisdom is based on the reality of the risen Christ. Science cannot give us eternal life. Jesus can.

The gospel backs up Paul's thought. It tells us about the ten bridesmaids, five of whom were wise and five foolish. The wise ones lived as true followers of the risen Christ, the five foolish ones did not. At Jesus' return at end-time the five wise bridesmaids will be rewarded with eternal life, whereas the five foolish ones will be excluded from it.

Let us not allow this scientific age of ours to turn us away from seeking the true wisdom who is Jesus. Science can search out ways for better material welfare. But Jesus leads us into fullness of life with the Father, thus making our life on earth the richer and our life hereafter complete. This is the much higher quest.

1. Why can't material goods give us full happiness?
2. Reflect on these words of St. Augustine: "My heart, O God is made for thee and will not rest until it rests in thee."
3. How is Jesus the way to true wisdom?
4. What word or phrase from the readings will you carry with you this week?

Thirty-third Sunday in Ordinary Time

Proverbs 31:10-13, 16-18, 20, 26, 28-31
1 Thessalonians 5:1-6
Matthew 24:36, 25:14-30

Life Is a Team Affair

In the sports section of the daily newspaper, you can often find an account of a coach who attributes his success to a good team spirit as well as to the efforts of each individual player. Conversely, a coach whose team consistently loses will say, "There's no team spirit. My players haven't got their hearts in the game."

Keep this example in mind as you take up the readings for this Sunday, for Christians are also a team. We are chosen by God to assist in the process of bringing all human beings to the fullness of life. Could there possibly be a greater challenge?

In the first reading the author of Proverbs praises married women for the great part they play in the faith challenge. "A capable wife, who can find her? She is far more precious than jewels. The heart of her husband trusts in her.... She does him good, and not harm, all the days of her life.... She opens her hand to the poor, and reaches out her hands to the needy."

Where do you find such a wife? Just look. She is in your neighbourhood. You meet her every day. Oh, she isn't perfect. She has her faults. But her heart is solid gold. She richly deserves our praise and gratitude. Moreover, she has a true team spirit and works night and day to help others. A good husband, too, is an indispensable part of that team. That is why in the Book of Ruth we read: "The Lord grant that you may find security [and love], each of you in the house of your husband" (Ruth 1:9).

In the second reading Paul praises his Thessalonian converts for their awareness about end-time. He doesn't have to convince them of its nearness, but only encourage them to greater watchfulness. "You are all children of light," he says to them, and continues: "We are not of the night or of darkness. So then let us not fall asleep as others do, but let us keep awake and be sober."

We know that this world won't last forever. It's a temporary arena. But in it a most serious game is being played, a game that may end at any moment, with the score remaining set for all eternity. Hence, like the Thessalonians, we are to "keep awake and be sober."

The gospel recounts the familiar parable of the talents. "A man, going on a journey, summoned his slaves and entrusted his property to them; to one he gave five talents, to another two, and to another one." On returning from abroad he praises those who used their talents wisely and condemns those who did not.

To the wise user of the talent the master says, "Well done, good and trustworthy slave; you have been trustworthy in a few things, I will put you in charge of many things; enter into the joy of your master." To the one who didn't use his talent at all, the master says, "As for this worthless slave, throw him into the outer darkness, where there will be weeping and gnashing of teeth."

The clock is ticking, but it won't always be. It may stop at any moment. This keeps us on our toes. It causes us to pause and ask ourselves whether we are using our talents to the full and using them for the sake of the kingdom.

1. How are Christians part of a team?
2. In what ways are we constantly reminded of how short life is?
3. What are your talents? How can you use them to help others?
4. What word or phrase from the readings will you carry with you this week?

Christt the King

Ezekiel 34:11-12, 15-17
1 Corinthians 15:20-26, 28
Matthew 25:31-46

A Shepherd in Our Midst

Our present world is without precedence.
For the first time in history, our world has
become a global village. When anything signifi-
cant takes place, the entire world knows of it
within minutes of its happening. All important
events are instantly world events.

To live in today's unfolding world, we need
help. So we turn to God's words in the readings
for this last Sunday of the liturgical year.

In the first reading, Ezekiel speaks out: "Thus
says the Lord God: I myself will search for my
sheep.... I will rescue them from all the places to
which they have been scattered.... I will bind up
the injured, and I will strengthen the weak."

Paul, too, comes to our aid: "Christ has been
raised from the dead.... As all die in Adam, so
all will be made alive in Christ." Thus we have
the wisdom and strength to shape our own lives,
and at the same time be a good influence to
thousands around us.

The gospel spells out the principal way we
are to live out our lives: by loving one another.
This was the first thing the pagan world noticed
about Christians. It should be the same today. In
Christ we have true wisdom, but a wisdom clothed
in love.

Through his death and resurrection, Jesus breathed new life into our world: a resurrection life, a life of unsurpassable strength and wisdom.

We are thus people of hope. We witness to the world with lives filled with the strength of Christ. We know that one day worldly powers will cease to be. Christ will return in glory to usher in the unending kingdom of God, the splendour and glory of which we cannot imagine.

1. How do you see today's world?
2. Reflect on Paul's words on how Jesus destroyed death.
3. Share your reaction to Matthew's "last judgment" scene (the only one in the Bible).
4. What word or phrase from the readings will you carry with you this week?

Also available from Novalis

Preparing for Sunday
Exploring the Readings for Year B

Preparing for Sunday
Exploring the Readings for Year C

The Living with Christ Sunday Missal

The *Living with Christ Sunday Missal* helps Catholics prepare for and participate more fully in the Sunday liturgy. Contains complete readings and mass texts, as well as selected hymns, for all Sundays and feast days. The perfect companion to *Preparing for Sunday*!

To order, call 1-800-387-7164
or visit our Web site:
www.novalis.ca

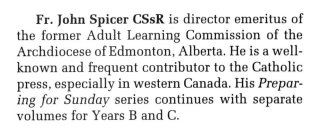

Fr. John Spicer CSsR is director emeritus of the former Adult Learning Commission of the Archdiocese of Edmonton, Alberta. He is a well-known and frequent contributor to the Catholic press, especially in western Canada. His *Preparing for Sunday* series continues with separate volumes for Years B and C.